W9-AAC-805

TO THE BREAK OF DAWN

WILLIAM JELANI COBB

TO THE BREAK OF DAWN

A Freestyle on the Hip Hop Aesthetic

New York University Press • *New York and London*

For Don-Dee & Deb: The Best Man & Woman

NEW YORK UNIVERSITY PRESS
New York and London
www.nyupress.org

Library of Congress Cataloging-in-Publication Data
Cobb, William Jelani.
To the break of dawn : a freestyle on the hip hop aesthetic / William Jelani Cobb.
p. cm.
Includes bibliographical references and index.
ISBN–13: 978–0–8147–1670–0 (cloth : alk. paper)
ISBN–10: 0–8147–1670–9 (cloth : alk. paper)
1. Hip-hop. I. Title.
ML3918.R37C63   2006
782.421649—dc22   2006029844

New York University Press books are printed on acid-free paper,
and their binding materials are chosen for strength and durability.

Manufactured in the United States of America

10 9 8 7 6 5 4 3 2 1

In spite of and because of marginal status, a powerful, indigenous vernacular tradition has survived, not unbroken, but unbowed, a magnet, a focused energy, something with its own logic, rules and integrity connecting current developments to the past. An articulate, syncretizing force our artists have drawn upon, a force sustaining both individual talent and tradition.

—John Edgar Wideman

You criticize our methods
Of how we make records
You said it wasn't art
So now we're gonna rip you apart

—Stetsasonic, "Talking All That Jazz"

Contents

Microphone Check

An Intro

That was us: the sweat-baptized, blue-light basement apostles of the breakbeat. We, the b-boy delegates of our five-borough universe, eyes hidden beneath baseball caps pulled low, uniformed in ?Guess, Kangol, and Adidas Olympic Team training gear. Our ranks cued *waaay* back to the subway lines that had delivered us to this place: Union Square, the nightspot deriving its name from the section of Manhattan where it was located. If you came from around our way, South Queens, specifically, then you gathered your tribe at 163rd Street and Hillside Ave and took the E to Lexington. Then you caught the downtown #6 to 14th Street, which delivered you to the far end of the Square.

At the front you encountered Muscle D, a brother swollen to a rippled abstraction, barely contained by his nylon tees and capable of *literally* moving the crowd. Down below was a consecrated dance-floor, the theater for our repertoire of movements: the Wop, the Rambo, the Fila, the Biz, the Prep. The true disciple could tell you that Rakim was there, the headlining act on the opening night at Union Square. That disciple would know that Jazzy Jeff & the Fresh Prince were to be the second act. Or that Biz-Markie rolled up in that spot on the reg, self-advertising with the boldfaced B-I-Z emblazoned on his cap—as if he was worried you would mistake him for Kool Moe Dee. You would remember the smell of it, if you had ever been there, the blunt-heavy air mixed with sweat, leather, Polo cologne, and some other indefinable element—a calibrated cool, perhaps—that we were so filled with that it must have seeped from our pores into the atmosphere also.

This is my romantic memory of the distant past. But the charitable will indulge my personal mythologizing for a moment.

1

The truth is that we seldom understand what era we are living in until that era is over. At the time I thought I was merely experiencing a hot moment in Manhattan, but across the span of two decades it has aged into . . . something else. A mental placeholder for a hundred other forgotten memories. The signpost for an innocence that long ago disappeared into history. The space that was Union Square is now a pet store, one of those national chains hustling overpriced canine couture. Our Benetton-and-Kangol gear has long fallen into disfashion and our once-young delegates to the five-borough assembly are now men and women approaching middle age.

And still something of it remains real.

There is an inventory of rhymes, some over twenty years old, that remain cataloged and stored in my memory. I can replay, line for line, Kool G. Rap's classic "Poison," or the infamous battle between Kool Moe Dee and Busy Bee. Name a track and I can tell you where I was when I heard it for the first time. "Rapper's Delight," the Sugar Hill Gang, 1979, a yellow house on 200th Street and Hollis Avenue. "Lights, Camera, Action," the Treacherous Three, 1982, basement apartment on Foch Avenue, off 142nd Street. "Sucker MCs," Run DMC, 1983, on the 8th-grade senior trip at a roller rink on the north side of town. "Ego Tripping," Ultra Magnetic MCs, Union Square, 1986. "Rebel without a Pause," Public Enemy, corner of Linden and Merrick boulevards, 1987.

In the ultimate equation, place and time don't matter, though—the book of Rakim teaches that it ain't where you from, it's where you at. But a brother still has love for the local. On the streets of South Queens, New York, in the mid-80s we honed verbal skills, traded our elementary freestyles, and chased after reputations for lyrical flow. At the part of Hollis Avenue that runs past the park on 205th Street, they used to steal power from the street lights and throw illegal jams back when Hollis Crew and Southside Posse were still civil warring. At I.S. 238, on Hillside and 179th Street, an eighth-grade nemesis named James Todd Smith handed me his autograph, saying that he would be famous one day. The signature read simply: *Cool J*—this was in the days before he prefaced his name with the Double Ls. Along Farmers Boulevard cats used to get their rhyme skills (and chins) tested on the Square. Liberty Avenue was where some of the illest did their dirt and whose residents always rolled deep to the shows at Club Encore.

Hip hop culture is a four-legged stool, its artistic pillars of deejay-ing, graffiti art, rapping, and b-boying coming into existence in rapid succession in the early 1970s and each influencing the ways in which the other evolved. In those early days, before artistic apartheid took hold, it was nothing for a rapper to moonlight as a graffiti artist or for a b-boy to also be known for ripping microphones. Long before low-wattage celebrities thought to *brand* or *cross-promote* themselves, artists were rapping and tagging graffiti under the same alias as to ensure that one's rep received its maximum dissemination.

Recognize: before middle-aged pundits started lamenting hip hop's "values," before rappers became unpaid boosters for the booze du jour, before ice was anything but frozen water, there was this: two turntables and a microphone. Before hip hop was old enough to see over the dashboard of America, the battles weren't between rappers in different time zones—it was all about inter-borough strife back then. Them Brooklyn cats had it in for the brothers from uptown; Bronx heads were constantly flexing on Brooklynites and *nobody* was feeling Queens. I remember when deejays at spots like Union Square and the Latin Quarter would ask if Queens was in the house as a semi-joke. Asking if Brooklyn was in the house was always a rhetorical question. In those days, our Kazal-goggled, black bomber-wearing assemblies kept our mouths shut fearing larceny from the Bed-Stuy, Harlem, South Bronx axis of evil. To cut to the quick: Queens was known for getting played.

Run & them changed that though.

I speak of the trio that put Queens—a borough that isn't even com-pletely on the New York City subway map—on the musical one. Kick-ing open the doors for acts like LL Cool J, MC Shan, Salt-N-Pepa, Kool G. Rap, Main Source, Nas, Ja Rule, and 50 Cent, they were responsible for transforming Queens status from that of cultural pariah to hip hop epicenter. For a good bloc of the music's history, between "King of Rock" and KRS-One's loathsome drive-by "The Bridge Is Over," Queens was officially running shit. These cats helped make it (slightly) safer to be from the city's largest borough and represent at hip hop shows. That Run, D, and the late scratch technician Jam Master Jay—the first legitimate superstars of the new music—would straight up claim Hollis, Queens, on wax all but reversed the previous borough-pecking order. These are small things in the grand flow of life and history, but they held import at the time. These were our battles until time and life delivered more weighty concerns onto our shoulders and then the music would reflect those new realities too.

Before we arrive at the mandatory Fanon quote, let us state the obvious: hip hop has, in the course of three decades, become the dominant form of youth culture on earth. It has ridden a tidal wave of American hegemony to the farthest expanses of the globe, carrying with it the complex, incomplete, and contradictory visions of those who created it as simultaneously the richest class of exploited people in world. Hip hop is culture. Hip hop is politics. Hip hop is economics. And it is something additional and unnamed. And now the Fanon: *Each generation must, from relative obscurity, discover its mission. It will either fulfill it or betray it.*

Hip hop is so central to the development of the post–civil rights generation of black people that it's nearly impossible to separate the music from our politics, economic realities, gains, and collective shortcomings. When I first heard Public Enemy's insurrection theme song "Black Steel in the Hour of Chaos" I literally did not know it was legal to speak such words on the radio. The distant echoes of the *Nation of Millions* album have been *reverberating* ever since. It was partly responsible for my dawning interest in the history of black peoples scattered throughout the world wholesale between the fifteenth and nineteenth centuries.

Each generation is imbued with its own unique moments of collective understanding, moments frozen in history when a sprawling set of people watched an iota, a fragment, or a vast chunk of their innocence slip away. In the case of those of us in the so-deemed "hip hop generation," our where-were-you moments were almost universally framed by hip hop narrative. The Rodney King beating and subsequent Los Angeles Riots—all but predicted and pre-narrated by Ice Cube's warning on *Amerikkka's Most Wanted* that the LAPD's role was "to serve, protect and break a nigga's neck." The horrors of September 11 bore an eerie resemblance to Rakim's Nostradamus-like tale of urban terrorism on "Casualties of War." The deaths of cornerstone artists Tupac Shakur and Notorious B.I.G. stole away a different kind of innocence from a generation that already been deemed cynical and lacking in idealism. That their deaths came to be seen in some quarters as "assassinations" on par with those of Malcolm or King illustrated not only how blurred the definitions of celebrity and leadership have become since the civil rights era, but also how few imaginative leaders have been cultivated since then. In their wake, charismatic artists were mistaken for political leadership. For me, the murders of musicians placed the sad dilemmas of black America in high relief: after a century that witnessed the rise of Jim Crow, lynching, black migration, slumification, Vietnam, incarceration, dissolving families, crack, and AIDS, African Americans—on the verge of a new millennium—were now killing each other over poetry.

That reckoning led me to stop listening to hip hop for almost four years believing it to be what I called "the soundtrack to self-inflicted genocide." The music that first articulated my understanding of the world around me had gone from obscure to ubiquitous; it had simultaneously become powerful and useless. I understood what Common had been metaphorically lamenting on "I Used to Love H.E.R" when he rhymed

I see her in commercials
She's universal
She used to only kick it
With the inner city circle

That remained the state of affairs until I was dragged to a Roots concert in late 2000. The dense crowd that had committed entire albums to memory, the hoodies and baseball caps, the antiseptically white Nikes, the freon cool, the absolutely kinetic vibe and the unrelenting heat of the performance that night. This was hip hop. This was truth. Over the course of that two-hour set, I came to remember hip hop had once been affirming, that it had once actually *been* real and hadn't needed to obsess over insecure cliches like "keeping it real." In the end, it was the pure lyrical genius of figures like Black Thought, Mos Def, Talib Kweli, Pharoahe Monch, and Common that led me to re-engage with hip hop on the level of art—even as my evolving humanist politics put me at odds with much of the form's content. To cut to the quick, it was a gradual understanding that hip hop was both an aesthetic statement and a political one, that the music was, in Mos Def's terms, *Black on Both Sides.*

Dig through the volumes of writing about hip hop and what emerges is one black side. The growing literature on hip hop features a thousand different spins on the theme of music as a social politic. And for good reason. In the space of a single generation, hip hop has evolved from the shunned expressions of disposable people into the dominant cultural idiom of youth globally. Rappers have literally gone from being maligned street poets to being A-list Hollywood stars, recording industry executives, film producers, and running up the score on their opponents in the culture wars. Hip hop has highlighted the black impulse toward verbal and musical invention and, at the same time, turned the most problematic, despair-riddled elements of American life into purchasable entertainment. The hip hop industry is largely responsible for the global re-dispersal of stereotypical visions of black sexuality, criminality, material-obsession, violence, and social detachment. That one can fly halfway around the world and be greeted in the Czech Republic by young men who speak no English, but regard you with a high-five and say "What up, Nigga?" is a bitterly ironic testament to the power and appeal of African American culture in the age of high capitalism.

But at the same time, hip hop is not fundamentally a political movement—no matter how many political implications the music and its mass marketing have. In 1926 Langston Hughes, as he rebelled against the artistic strictures prescribed by *official* black leadership, wrote the essay "Negro Artist and the Racial Mountain," in which he pointed out that art and politics have had a notoriously rocky marriage. Hip hop is many things, but most prominently it is a musical movement cornerstoned by a tradition of verbal creativity. That is to say that hip hop is not only a contribution to black music, but also black language arts. Future anthologies of black literature will need hip hop citations and future students will (if they haven't already) turn in term papers with titles like "Metaphor and Simile in the Works of Lauryn Hill and Langston Hughes."

And on this last point, we have to be clear. Much has been made of the multiculturalization of hip hop in the years since it first rumbled out of the Bronx. On one level, this is historically inaccurate in that hip hop *began* as a multicultural movement. It represented the artistic communion between young Latinos, West Indians, and post-migration African Americans. In the 1970s the South Bronx became to this diverse collection of peoples what Paris was in the 1930s to the diverse body of peoples who had been colonized by the French and who eventually created the Negritude Movement. It was to these people what London was to the body of Caribbean and African intellectuals who met and organized the anticolonial movements of the 1940s. And it was what Harlem had been in the 1920s, when a similar group of peoples—West Indians like

Claude McKay, Southern migrants like Zora Neale Hurston, and Latinos like Arthur Schomburg—created the artistic movement that came to known as the Harlem Renaissance.

But this new multiculturalism is global and international and also refers obliquely to the vast numbers of white Americans who now participate in the culture. Hip hop, we are told, has gone universal. And yet, my references to this as a black art form are intentional. Seventy-eight years ago, at the height of the Harlem Renaissance, the sage W. E. B. Du Bois remarked that "As soon as true Negro art emerges, it is said 'That person did this because he is an American, not because he is a Negro; as a matter of fact there is no such thing as a Negro." Such is the case with the ongoing perceptions of jazz and blues as quintessentially "American" artforms—decreasingly owing their existence to the social quarantine of Jim Crow and the aesthetic laboratories that generations of Negro artists created within it. By this logic, Rakim, Jay-Z, MC Lyte, KRS-One, Lauryn Hill, OutKast, Scarface, Ice Cube, Common, and Snoop Dogg are Americans, not Negroes—and Eminem must be the President.

The truth is that it is possible to be both specific and universal simultaneously. The legions of mic-grabbing rhyme spitters in Germany, Japan, France, and Amsterdam are no more contrary to the black roots of hip hop than Leontyne Price was a threat to the Italian roots of opera. Hip hop is literally a product of the African Diaspora—with breakdancing owing its existence to the Afro-Brazilian martial art form of Capoeira, deejaying growing from the genius of Caribbean migrants to the United States, and MCing evolving at the crossroads of a number of verbal traditions. I use the term black as an—admittedly awkward—reference to that body of Africa-derived cultures, specifically those of North America and the Caribbean, and the term African American to describe the group of Africa-descended peoples in the United States.

And now a confession: of the four pillars of hip hop—breaking, graffiti art, deejaying, and rapping—I am focusing on the craft of the MC, the most widely recognized of hip hop participants. There are volumes to be spoken on the artistic skill of the turntablist; the re-made acrobatics of the b-boy, who fashioned a new form from the Capoeira martial art created by stolen Africans in Brazil; and the alphabetic abstraction of the graffiti tagger. But I'll leave that for future writers.

I'm talking specifically about MCs in these pages, not the general category of *rappers*. Every MC raps, but not every rapper is an MC. Truth told, there are scores of successful rappers who have never *met* an actual MC. Like Madison-Avenued, focus-grouped novelties, rappers are created in accord with the reigning flavor of the nanosecond. Right about now, most rappers exist as living product placements, their gear, their rides, their whole set-up as deliberately schemed as that can of Coke downed by your favorite action hero before he splits to do battle with the special-effected forces of evil. Only the mad niche-marketers of American hypercapitalism could conceive of the modern rap video— basically a commercial in which products advertise other products. It would be easy to freestyle on the soul-nullifying effects of capitalism on art, but the point is that the music, *the art* of hip hop, has to be understood as distinct from the cellophane-shrouded rap products sitting in the music bin at Wal-Mart.

Flip on your TV, turn on the radio, open a magazine and there's a good chance that there's a rapper floating on your medium of choice. An MC, though, is a whole 'nother thing entirely. Microphone Controller, Mic Checker, Master of Ceremonies, Mover of Crowds, in hip hop, the letters MC are as undefined as the X that followed Malcolm's name.

The genealogy of the MC runs all the way back to hip hop's fetal days when the DJ was at the center of the culture and the Master of Ceremonies was essentially a sideman. The group was called Grand Master Flash and the Furious Five for a reason: Flash's eye-blurring hand speed and slick scratches had made him a boulevard celebrity long before the heads on the boulevard got wise to the vocal talents of Cowboy, Melle Mel, Rakim, Mr. Ness, or Kid Creole. The DJ selected the array of sounds that the masses would move to, operated literally as the architect of a vibe. The DJ's primacy—and the MC's secondary status—had started to change by the time you got to groups identified by a single common name like the Cold Crush Brothers or the Fearless Four. The situation was clearly reversed when you got to Run DMC & Jam Master Jay—two rappers and a DJ who were more commonly referred to as just Run DMC.

The difference between a rapper and an MC is the difference between smooth jazz and John Coltrane, the difference between studio and unplugged. Or, to cop a line from Alice Walker, the difference between indigo and powder blue. Nelly is a rapper; KRS-One is an MC twenty-five hours a day. Lauryn Hill is, straight up and down, an MC's MC; the Fresh Prince was an MC; Will Smith is a rapper. Nas has been an MC since he breathed his first; P. Diddy and Master P. are rappers down to their DNA.

The rapper is judged by his ability to move units; the measure of the MC is the ability to move crowds. The MC gets down to his task with only the barest elements of hip hop instrumentalization: two turntables and a microphone. On that level, the Miami basspreneur Luke, who didn't even necessarily *rhyme*, was closer to being an MC than Hammer, who did rhyme—or at least attempted to. The MC writes his own material. The MC would still be writing his own material even if he didn't have a record deal. A rapper without a record deal is a commercial without a timeslot. Regarding the difference between rapper and MC, KRS breaks it down like this:

> *A dope MC is a dope MC*
> *With or without a record deal, all can see*
> *And that's what KRS is, son*
> *I'm not the run of the mill 'cause for the mil' I don't run*

Still, you can get yourself in trouble thinking that art is easily categorized. Jay-Z, Eminem, Notorious B.I.G., 50 Cent, Tupac Shakur, DMX, and LL Cool J are all MCs *who are also rappers*, meaning they have managed to exist within the commercial arena while maintaining their integrity as artists. To avoid confusion, I use the term *rapper* as a general reference to hip hop vocalists—and *MC* when I mean to connote that specific brand of verbal marksmen who were forged in the crucible of the street jam, the battle, and the off-the-top-of-the-dome freestyle.

There has emerged over the last ten years a body of hip hop music criticism from the pages of niche outlets like *Source, XXL, Vibe,* the now-defunct *Blaze,* hip hop websites, and mainstream music magazines like *Spin* and *Rolling Stone*—but the criticism most often deals with how well a particular rapper or group of rappers met commonly accepted standards for the form, not the exploration of those standards themselves. My intent here is to understand hip hop as an *aesthetic*, not necessarily a social movement. To deal, in other words, with the art on its own terms. The issues of sexism, violence, homophobia, and materialism have been raised and thoroughly treated by other writers. This is not a history of hip hop, though it necessarily contains historical elements. The history of the music has been chronicled in songs, magazines, books, and websites. The history and politics of the art form as well as the generation that created it have been chronicled in works such as Bakari Kitwana's *Hip Hop Generation,* Jeff Chang's *Can't Stop, Won't Stop,* Ego Trip's *Book of Rap Lists,* Gwendolyn Pough's *Check It While I Wreck It,* Tricia Rose's *Black Noise,* and Mark Neal and Murray Foreman's *That's the Joint,* among others. There is always room for additional voices, but hip hop's political and social elements can at last lay claim to a substantive body of literature.

So this book aims for a different kind of conversation. It is a treatment of themes in the music and culture—some of which have historical threads. *To the Break of Dawn* is an extended liner note on the artistic evolution of rap music and its relationship to earlier forms of black expression. It is also not meant to be exhaustive. There are plenty of rappers you won't find discussed in these pages. Hip hop is diverse and subdividing by the minute. Still it is worthwhile to distill commonalities in the craft of rapping up to this particular point.

This book is divided into five sections: "The Roots" traces hip hop's relationship to the ancestral forms of expression, particularly blues and the oral tradition. It takes direct issue with those mumble-mouthed and cliché assertions that hip hop is less than a full descendant of the traditions of African American and Diasporan cultures in the United States. "The Score" charts hip hop's aesthetic evolution from its inception in the South Bronx through its standing as a complex, multi-layered music that has expanded enough to actually have regional and stylistic sub-genres. "Word of Mouth" examines the cultural and literary elements that are the foundation of MC culture. In hip hop we find the practice of the entire palette of poetic techniques; this part charts the innovative ways in which varieties of rhyme, metaphor, simile, assonance, and alliteration are used inside the art form. "Asphalt Chronicles" details the importance of the storytelling tradition within hip hop. Hip hop, more than any other popular descendant of the blues, places emphasis upon narration. The ways in which story is used within hip hop sheds light on both the genre's musical roots and its relationship to the tradition of black autobiography in this country. The final part, "Seven MCs," looks at the contributions of seven artists to the evolution of the music. This is not one of those tired "top 100" lists that seem to be the mainstay of magazines and cable music shows, but a look at what each of these artists brought—or brought out—in the music. It is possible to understand the music through the lens of an individual's body of work and that is what this final part seeks to achieve.

To the Break of Dawn is my attempt to enter this dialogue; it examines the aesthetic, stylistic, and thematic evolution of hip hop from its inception in the South Bronx to the present era of distinctly regional sub-divisions and styles. Back when I was a word-scribbling acolyte trying to make subject and verb agree, I was given the age-old advise to "write what you know." And what I knew was hip hop. The first words I ever wrote seriously were rhymes—material for my stalled adolescent career as South Queens's own MC Trate, the self-professed Freestyle King. My first conscious goal when I started writing essays was to sound on a page the way Chuck D sounded on a record. This book reflects my particular relationship to the art form. Although I've heard and dug hip hop in all its multi-regional diversity, I am, at my core, an old-school East Coast cat—a reality that the reader will likely note in these pages.

My sincerest hope is that this book remains true to the art form that first introduced me to creative genius. In the years since the movie *Brown Sugar* premiered, it has become cliché to ask *When did you fall in love with hip hop?* But the question still warrants a response. My answer is this: from the first second I heard the first rhyme delivered over the first break beat. I loved it from the time I was a heavy-lidded ten-year-old struggling to stay up to 2 A.M. to tape *The Mr. Magic Show* on WHBI to my present standing as a man just old enough to begin idealizing his youth. To cop a line from Common, I used to love her. And twenty-five years after that first blessed encounter, despite numberless frustrations with what she has become, I still do.

I

The Roots

It begins with the words: mic check. The MC counts it off, one, two, one, two, before running down his pedigree: I go by the name of the one MC Lingo of the mighty Black Ops and we came here tonight to get y'all open . . . *In the MC's ritual, the next task is the demographic survey—*Is Brooklyn in the house?*—even though he knows the answer; always knew the answer 'cause the answer is always the same. Brooklyn is as ubiquitous as bad luck. There's a cat behind him on the ones and twos; his head cocked to the left, headphones cradled between ear and shoulder. He has the fingertips of his left hand resting on a 12" instrumental, the right on the cross-fader. His MC gets four bars to drop it a capella, after that he comes behind him with Michael Viner's* Apache. *A measure beforehand, he'll idle with some prelim scratches to let the crowd know what's coming next. And if his boy got skills enough, if the verbal game is tight enough, that right there will be the kinetic moment, that blessed split-second when beat meets rhyme. The essence of hip hop. Come incorrectly, though, and the heads in attendance will let you know that too. In hip hop, subtlety is considered a character flaw. In hip hop, it is a moral wrong to allow a wack MC to exist unaware of his own wackness. The DJ hits with the track, the MC wraps his tongue around a labyrinth of syllables, and don't have to chase his breath. We came here tonight to get y'all open . . .* He knows when it's done correctly because the heads start to nod in affirmation.

ORIGINS OF THE BOOM BAP

For those still concerned with the terms laid down by Webster, art is defined as this: 1. Conscious arrangement of sounds, colors, forms, movement, or other elements in a way that affects the aesthetic sense: 2. A specific skill in adept performance, held to require the exercise of intuitive faculties: 3. Production of the beautiful. The MC, despite the grumblings of various antique-aged gripers, is a modern incarnation of the

13

black verbal artist, whose lineage runs way back to the black preacher, the bluesman, and the boulevard griot. Some critics, detractors, and, in the tongue of the boulevard, *haters*, would have it that hip hop fell from the sky—untouched by any preceding black art form. We're to believe that the backward sex politics, the materialism, the violence that characterize some hip hop are unique products of post–civil rights black culture and that the art—if it can even be called that—bears no resemblance to the now-classic forms of jazz and blues. We hear such nonsensical claims from artists like Wynton Marsalis and Stanley Crouch, who, as jazz and blues heads, know better—or really ought to.

Their music began in the gutter. The sounds rumbled up from the terrorized Delta topsoil and the people the color of it, the music of the bayou ho' houses now gone Lincoln-Center respectable. Rock and roll, now enshrined as a sacrament of the boomer generation, derived its name from the black street-corner terminology for sex. And hip hop grows from that same seed, germinating in those same urinated alleys, only nine hundred miles further north. The hood, the barrio, the broken precincts of the city breathed life into hip hop in the 1970s, but from top to bottom, the music was in communion with older principles not only in terms of its politics, but also its *aesthetics*.

For the unschooled, the concept that hip hop even has an aesthetic is alien; that there is a sonic distinction between the great MC and his wack counterpart is lost on most of the consuming public and the genre's detractors alike. Because hip hop is discussed most often on the level of commerce and politics, but rarely on the level of art, it's easy to miss the fact that the form has its own aesthetic, its own standards and measures—this aesthetic is idiosyncratic and unique, but is also built on earlier forms. At its core, hip hop's aesthetic contains three components: music, or "beats," lyrics, and "flow"—or the specific way in which beats and lyrics are combined.

The heart of the art of hip hop is how the MC does what he does—the specific catalog of trade trickery he uses to get his people open. And just as the MC is at the center of hip hop, his tools—verbal craft, articulation, improvisation—are at the center of black cultures. The pedigree runs deep. It connects that dreadlocked, mic-gripping orator to the tradition of black verbal gamesmanship that starts with the black preacher, whom Du Bois reckoned with in *Souls of Black Folk* as "the most unique personality created by the Negro on American soil." Zora Neale

Hurston identified the preacher as the first black artist in America, the poet who made helped make the absurd world intelligible.

> Our preachers are talented men even though many of them are barely literate. The masses do not read literature, do not visit theaters, nor museums of the fine arts. The preacher must satisfy their beauty-hunger himself. He must be a poet and an actor and possess a body and a voice . . . It is not admitted as such by our "classes." Only James Weldon Johnson and I give it praise. It is utterly scorned by the "Niggerati." But the truth is, the greatest poets among us are in our pulpits and the greatest poetry has come out of them. It is merely not set down. It passes from mouth to mouth as in the days of Homer.

James Baldwin, boy preacher emeritus, copped his long, elegant, multi-claused sentence style from the oracular rhythms of the black church and broke this down for all posterity when he said:

> The Black preacher, since the church was the only Civilized institution that we were permitted—separately—to enter, was our first warrior, *terrorist*, or *guerrilla. He* said that freedom was real—that *we* were real. *He* told us that *trouble don't last always. He* told us that our children and elders were sacred, when the Civilized were spitting on them and hacking them to pieces, in the name of God and in order to keep on making money.

Recognize that the African, stolen and shackled, scorned and rejected, was dropped into a textual culture from an oral tradition where articulation was paramount. Circumstance and eight weeks on the Atlantic had placed the inheritors of highly inflective West African tongues into an environment of linguistic hostility. Not only were their indigenous languages derided and outlawed, but the very nature of the *creole* English they spoke was cited as a mark of inferiority. And it is unspeakably difficult to be a poet in a language that is hostile to your existence. Even more, one can only speculate at the vast ideas and shades of meaning that the newly enslaved could find no way to express in the slave-master's vocabulary. The old maxim teaches that "art is a technique of communication," but the converse also holds true. It was for this reason that the black preacher, the only individual granted even limited vocal carte blanche, would emerge also as the ancestral black artist.

And given that relationship to the spoken word, literacy could easily be secondary in the preacher's art. Articulation in a foreign tongue—one that was learned in bondage and taught solely as a means of conveying orders—is in and of itself a form of mastery. A slave exists to obey commands, but only a *human* commands language. American law and American deed defined the African as a non-entity, the extension of the master's will and possessor of nothing, but an articulator owns language—and a share (however small) of the ideas that those arrayed syllables represent. It was no coincidence that a slave holy man's apocalyptic vision of black angels slaying white angels in the sky prefaced the uprising that planted fear in the slaveholding soul. Nat Turner. August 21, 1831. Fifty-seven of them—man, woman, and infant—left dead in his wake. A sermon of sorts.

The African, enslaved in a land of strange deeds and customs and shackled into a new language, made speech into a metaphor for identity. If English vocabulary was mandatory, its grammatical roots were to remain West African and the lexicon spiced with the unforgotten words from home. The evolution of that *creole* may chart the evolving new world identity, but the issue at hand is how that ebonic fusion came to be used. The well-spoken word, in ways both subtle and vast, undermined the decree that the African was to possess nothing and thus preceded physical freedom. So, straight up: the preacher's central task was to open his mouth and rip it the best way he saw fit as a confirmation of the collective existence. The verbal strategy, the specific catalog of trade trickery employed by the preacher, laid down the parameters for his vocal heirs four hundred years down the line.

Listen for a minute and it becomes clear that the rapper is evaluated by many of the same criteria as the preacher: use of voice, timbre, timing, reference, and sub-reference. The preacher uses amen as a verbal stopgap the same way the old-school rapper used catch-phrases like "Yes, yes, y'all" or "It don't stop," etc. The preacher earns his or her keep by the call and the response; the rapper lives and dies by his skill at getting the crowd open. Generations of black secular singers have claimed the church as their first training ground, but what has gone unrecognized is that the rapper is their counterpart—the secular preacher, the sanctified exhorter whose skills have passed by cultural osmosis from the pulpit to the boulevard.

This is not to say that early MCs copped their styles directly from the local South Bronx preacher in the way that soul singers fell back on what they learned in choir practice. A host of verbal intermediaries exist between the preacher and the MC. But when you cut through all the *begats*, the preacher and the MC retain their family resemblance. Example: Melle Mel's percussive *rah* at the end of his verses is only degrees removed from the preacher's percussive *huh*—employed as an oral semicolon or period in the sermon. Or check Nelly's flow on the confectionery "Hot in Herre," Snoop Dogg's trademark drawled-out vowels, or Bone Thugs' fluid mic vocalism and their common, deliberately sing-songy cadences, which immediately recall the Baptist tradition of *hooping*—tap dancing on the perimeter between speech and song in a sermon.

The Reverend C.L. Franklin pointed out that the best *hoopers* were preachers who could also sing well—this from a man whose daughter Aretha would become the greatest soul singer of all time. The best MCs do not necessarily sing well, but absolutely possess a singer's understanding of time, nuance, and interpretation. Hooping—accompanied often by fragmentary organ riffs, or *samples*—is essentially a form of unrhymed rapping. Utilizing timing, meter, and inflection, it's the sermonic equivalent of the blank verse in Shakespeare's plays—rhymeless poetry presented in a prose format.

History is like viewing of a movie for the second time and gaining a vast new world of insights into the plot. Those who make history may or may not be wise to the full dimensions of their accomplishments because their lifetime is only the first screening. From the gate, the ancestral b-boys created a new musical history—even as they drew upon art that was already in existence as a resource for the art that they would create. In short, this "new" musical history was not and could not have been a clean break from the old one. MCing may have begun as a musical ad campaign for the deejay who ran the show, but the fundamental concept of pairing the rhymed verse with the hypnotism of bared percussion had been laid down way before that.

Of those multiple millions of Africans snatched from their indigenous contexts by the transatlantic slave trade, only some 6 percent arrived on the shores that would become the United States. Meaning that 94 percent of that displaced humanity found themselves immersed in the agricultural brutalities of Jamaica, Cuba, Brazil, Argentina, Nicaragua, Peru, Trinidad, Barbados, Surinam, Columbia, Haiti—the scattered localities of common bondage. Those same language dynamics played themselves out in each of these places, creating a network of

African-derived patois and political implications for the spoken word—which explains in extreme shorthand how dancehall and hip hop could come into existence as cousin cultures.

The African American and Caribbean American teenagers who found themselves building a new culture up in the South Bronx in 1974 shared four centuries of collective history that gave context to the art they created. They had come from the same boat, having merely departed at different stops. Nor was the fact that so many of the early b-boys were of Caribbean descent coincidental. The cornerstone deejays Kool Herc and Afrika Bambaataa are both of Jamaican descent and Grandmaster Flash is of Barbadian ancestry. Nor is it coincidental that the Caribbean had long established its parallel tradition of "dub poetry" or syncopated rhyme verse accompanied by percussion. Listen to the work of Linton Kwesi Johnson or Mutubaruka and the imprint of this tradition on hip hop becomes undeniable.

You could trace hip hop's roots back to scat, which gave literal expression to the concept that a sound could carry meaning irrespective of its relationship to formal language. You find hip hop in the poetry of Leopold Senghor and Aime Cesaire, the black bards who went from the Negritude literary movement they founded to formal leadership of their people in Senegal and Martinique. Hip hop's ancestry is James Weldon Johnson, the first black president of the NAACP, writing the lyrics for the Negro National Anthem, "Lift Ev'ry Voice and Sing." It is Marcus Garvey and W. E. B. Du Bois, the two colossal opponents of colonialism in Africa, both articulating the cause of the dispossessed in poetic verse. And Amiri Baraka's leadership in the Black Power political campaigns of Newark in 1972. The point is this: the art *is* the politic.

The relationship between the preacher and the rapper is one of both form and content. Think about that for a minute and you can damn-near write a sermon based on Mos Def's jewel "New World Water." It's impossible to ignore the prominence of water as a primary motif in black spiritual culture—from the debilitated Gospel pleas to be "washed white as snow" to the rebellion-coded double entendre "wade in the water," which referenced both baptism and escape routes from slavery. En route to issuing an injunction against the waste of natural resources, Mos Def drops the observation that "Fools done upset/the old man river/made him carry slave ships/and fed him dead niggers"—a line that echoes Amiri Baraka's reminder that "there is a railroad made from human bones at the bottom of the Atlantic." The water of the alleged new world was precisely what divided Jamestown from Benin, Santo Domingo from Oyo, Sao Paolo from Kannem Borno. And that same water is the eternal resting ground of black millions lost to the middle passage. Waters being fed dead Africans—cruel irony for descendants of cultures who understood that all life derived from and began in water, centuries before Western empirical intellect was made wise to that fact. Black folklore tells us of people who could walk on water—Africans who surveyed the new world real estate and opted to take the long haul back home by foot.

To the enslaved, though, to the African landlocked into American servitude, the waters rippled differently. For them, the spirituals' reference to "Crossing the River Jordan" functioned as a triple entendre: biblical allusion, figurative expression of crossing the meridian between North and South, and as literal direction toward an escape route. Forbidden to seek communion and connection with water-associated Orisha, Yemoja, Olucun, or Oshun, baptism was left to function as spiritual substitute—and became a factor in the Baptists' early success in recruiting black congregants.

Public Enemy made this link explicit with the preamble to the sonic anarchy of "Rebel without a Pause" by sampling Jesse Jackson preaching *Brothers and Sisters, I don't know what this world is coming to* . . . then comes an explosion of baritone and brimstone. And by the time you hear Chuck-D's "Up you mighty race" lyrical polemics, the point has been made: the rapper is finishing Jesse's sentence, literally picking up where the preacher left off. You could riff on the line of reasoning with the explicit biblical reference that Lauryn Hill brought to the table with *The Miseducation of Lauryn Hill* or the rough-hewn, avenue Christianity espoused by the late Notorious B.I.G., but the point is that the MC exists inside a broader, older vocal tradition. For the rappers gone sacred—Run and Mase, now turned Reverends Run and Mase—trading in throwback jerseys for pastoral robes mirrors a pivot that soul singers have been making for decades. And in so doing they've essentially put in for a transfer from one branch of black verbal art to its ancestral root. DMX's gravelly preacher-voice recalls the old traditions, from back in the times when men of God were still called *exhorters*. His debut *It's Dark and Hell Is Hot* is a seminar on the asphalt theology of the millennial street hood. No question, the rapper had turned exhorter when he offered an a capella prayer as the sixteenth track on his debut release:

You give me word and only ask that I interpret
And You give me eyes that I might recognize the serpent

There is an apocryphal tale that tells of DMX buying a Brooklyn church out of its back-tax debt, offering a blessing to the house of the Lord. The truth or falseness of the story is secondary: what matters is that the story was credible enough to be relayed. The MC replicates and remixes the craft of preaching, jacking one set of oratory tactics for application in the world of sin and concrete. To cut to the quick, there is more than a set of initials connecting C.L. Franklin to CL Smooth.

THE TRICKSTER BLUES

We listen to the MC and we hear the echo of the old-time revival ex-horters, but at the same time, the rapper is linked to a whole other side of the black aesthetic tradition—having copped key elements of the blues craft. Blues is at the corner of all American popular musics, but hip hop in particular descended from the blues tradition of orality. If the blues is the sound of a post-slave people in the social vacuum of the American South and the tale of that people on their way north, then en-coded within hip hop of the story of what happened once they arrived.

On one level, the bluesman paved the way for the rapper in that the blues brought calm recognition to the concept of human evil as a con-sequence of human existence. The blank-faced, cinema verité street nar-ration of the gangsta rapper could not have come into existence without the blues and its understanding of morality. Here we have no sacred, no secular because the bluesman grapples with a far older concept—that there is ultimately neither. The world simply *is*, period. Eons before postmodern literary critics were wise to this, blues people recognized that the world could be read as text, that the dirt road was a metaphor and the juke joint a temple to the prayers of the flesh. In short, that *life* could be its own holy book.

Gallons of ink have been spilled in attempts to define what the blues is—and what it *ain't* for that matter. Literary bluesman and musi-cian Ralph Ellison put it this way:

> The blues is an impulse to keep the painful details and episodes of a
> brutal existence alive in one's aching consciousness, to finger its

jagged grain, and to transcend it, not by the consolation of philosophy but by squeezing from it a near tragic, near-comic lyricism. As a form, the blues is an autobiographical chronicle of personal catastrophe expressed lyrically.

Caught in the existential staredown with abject circumstance, the blues artist pulls the only weapon available: a sharpened sense of irony, the simultaneous reckoning with the bitter and the sweet, the last-ditch laughter that staves off tears. That confrontation with the absurd contradictions of his own existence—the descendant of allegedly lazy people who were brought to another continent in order to work, member of an unclean race whose primary employment is in cleaning homes—was grist for the blues' hallmark irony, what we might call the trickster consciousness.

The trickster's ironic sensibility is a defining feature of the blues, where the hero is the down-and-out player who nevertheless carries an ace—or a razor, depending on the situation—tucked up his sleeve. This is apparent on the version of "Red House" recorded by Jimi Hendrix:

> There's a red house over yonder, that's where my baby stay
> Lord, there's a red house over yonder, that's where my baby stay
> I ain't been home to see my baby, in 99 and one half days.
>
> Wait a minute, somethin's wrong, this key don't fit the door
> Wait a minute somethin's wrong here, this key don't unlock the door
> I got a bad, bad feelin' my baby don't live here no more.
>
> I guess I'll go back over yonder, way over the hill
> I guess I'll go back over yonder, way up over that hill
> 'cause if my baby don't love me no more, I know her sister will.

Being down don't mean the same thing as being out and right here we see that getting left by one's woman ain't the same thing as being left *without* a woman. Albert King gave light to the same theme with the version of "Born Under a Bad Sign" he recorded in 1967. He sang:

> Born under a bad sign
> I been down ever since the day I could crawl

And if it wasn't for bad luck
I wouldn't have no luck at all.

Still, he ends up with the admission that "when I die a big-leg woman will carry me to my grave." High-octane spirits and well-curved women might well be the death of him, but if he's going out like that, he plans to shuffle off the mortal plane with the finest pallbearer you ever seen. And the loudly unstated point is that his cadaver is leaving with a finer woman than his peers got—and they still *alive*.

History spotlights violent resisters of slavery like Toussaint L'Ouverture, Nat Turner, and Zumbi dos Palmares, but the average slave, physically outnumbered or at least outgunned, could not always rely upon brute force resistance. Deception, Du Bois points out in *Souls of Black Folk*, is the natural defense of the weak against the strong. And deception is the primary weapon in the arsenal of the trickster. The trickster in most folklore traditions is not particularly strong physically but manages to outdo his foes with cunning and double-edged wit. Given the nature of the black relationship to the Western world, it makes sense that trickster tales are one of the folklore traditions that survived the middle passage and took root throughout the Diaspora in the form of Anansi, Brer Rabbit, and the Signifyin' Monkey. Among the Dogon of Mali, the trickster holds a primary cosmological significance:

> The Dogon imagination [uses] humor as an image of the creative necessity of disorder . . . laughter itself becomes a reversal of order for the revelation of deeper order, an abolition of time for the capture of time . . . Turns the world upside down so that it can proceed right side up.

Among the Yoruba, the trickster *orisha* Elegba is the master of the crossroads and fate. He is traditionally depicted as a child or an old man. Elegba opens and closes doors. Now look at the crossroads as they appear in blues as one of the most consistent references and double entendres in the form. For the blues artist, the itinerant bard of the newly dilated black world, the crossroads represent decision-making—a particularly important reference given the fact that the essence of slavery is the absence of mobility and the inability to make one's own decisions.

The crossroads is both geographic and metaphorical, an echo of the old trickster ways.

Westerners have conflated Elegba the trickster with their concept of the devil in the raw attempt to impose a good versus evil dichotomy on vastly more complex ways of understanding the world. To the wise, though, the trickster is neither good, nor evil, he simply *is*. The trickster's place in the blues, plus the secular emphasis of the form, gave rise to the epithet "devil music." Never mind the fact that it was in the crossroads where Robert Johnson allegedly sold his soul to the "devil" in exchange for mastery of his instrument. But the blues did not create the trickster—they simply gave him a new venue. The trickster ideal was in place in the pre-blues world of the slave. Bear in mind the old tale of the white woman who leaves the big house to inform her slaves that the terrible news they've heard is true—the North has, in fact, won the war. Slavery is over, she says, but if they're willing to stay on, they can create a world that is "just the same as it always was." Her slaves line up and dutifully inform her of how good a mistress she's been and how glad they'd be to remain in her service. The belle goes to bed with a light heart only to awake and find that there is not a single ex-slave in sight for miles. The world had, in fact, been turned upside down for centuries and the Janus-faced slave-trickster knew that deception and flight was the means of turning it right side up.

The blues artist must be willing to reckon with human frailty, the dead-broke, woman-gone existential zero-ness that has to be admitted before it can be transcended. In short, one must recognize one's frailty before it can be used to your advantage. But if the blues exist for the express purpose of alchemizing beauty from pain, hip hop is more often about swaggering in the face of it. Denying that pain is an element of its reality. Hip hop is that boxer who gets caught flush by the unseen right hand and then tells his antagonist that it didn't hurt—and the fact is, of course, that if it really didn't hurt he wouldn't feel the need to make that statement. With the exception of Mos Def's comic "Ms. Fat Booty" and Jay-Z's "Song Cry," the number of hip hop songs dealing substantively with a man whose woman has left could probably be counted on one hand. And even Jay-Z's effort tempered by his refrain "I can't see 'em coming out my eyes/So I gotta make this song cry." Now compare that to the soreness of the soul expressed in Ishman Bracey's "Trouble-Hearted Blues," where he laments

I don't believe I'm sinking
Believe what a hole I'm in
You don't believe I loved you
think what a fool I been.

Or Joe Pullum's 1934 lamentation in "Black Gal What Makes Your Head So Hard?" that

I woke up this morning
couldn't even get out my bed
I was just thinking about that black woman
And it almost killed me dead.

At the heart of hip hop's denial of the pain—a pain that is so openly voiced in the blues—is a different relationship to irony within the two musics. The trickster's ironic approach to life and power relations had resonance to the enslaved for obvious reasons: the trickster appears to be happy and harmless, traffics in deception, and disarms with a smile. The average rapper, though, would rather get shot than smile in public.

Hip hop doesn't place as high a premium on irony as its ancestral forms, particularly blues—even as it relies upon blues and the surrounding blues folklore for much of its material. This is not to say that hip hop is completely anti-ironic, simply that irony is not at the center of the hip hop ethos. That said, hip hop has precious little room for acknowledging pain in order to ultimately transcend it.

That absence of irony is why on nearly every album cover the rapper holds a murderer's grit on his face. Even comedic rappers tend to look serious as hell, half-glaring up from an oblique angle, as if smiling is a violation of a sacred MC credo. Irony is at the center of blues, however—it is, at its root, a music about existential despair that is deeply opposed to resignation or defeat. It's been pointed out more than once that blues was created just after slavery by the most oppressed segment of American society, but rarely do you encounter explicit discussion of race or racism within the lyrics—save brilliant queries like "What did I do to get so black and blue?" Blues grapples with the individual tragedy in full public view, an aesthetic habit that's absent from all but the most significant hip hop.

HEAR MY TRAIN A COMIN'

Fruit may not fall far from the tree, but it does, nonetheless, fall. While blues obsesses over the theme of mobility, hip hop is as local as a zip code. The constant blues references to crossroads, trains, and railroad tracks rise from the itinerant life at the turn of the century. Between 1920 and 1942, at least 293 blues songs about trains or railroads were recorded. This is the music of black wanderers exercising the newly granted right of mobility. And thus we encounter titles like "Goin' Away Blues," "So Many Roads, So Many Trains," "Crossroads Blues," and "Further On Up the Road." The blues tell us that

> *When a woman gets the blues*
> *She hangs her head and cries*
> *When a man gets the blues*
> *Lord, he grabs a train and rides.*

In hip hop, though, there are no references to highways or trains; railroads have been replaced by another central reference: the City. Or more specifically, the fractured territories known collectively as the Ghetto. Innumerable hip hop songs reference the term: Naughty By Nature's "Ghetto Bastard," Rakim Allah's "In the Ghetto" Nas's "Ghetto Prisoners," Talib Kweli's "Ghetto Afterlife," Lauryn Hill's "Every Ghetto, Every City," Dr. Dre's "The World Is a Ghetto," all allude to a socio-economic blind alley, a terrain defined by the lack of mobility of its residents. Scarface—formerly of the ensemble the Geto Boys—underscores this point on the single "On My Block," where he rhymes, "It's like the rest of the world don't exist/we stay confined to same spot we been livin' in." Jean Grae riffed on this same theme on "Block Party," imploring heads to "Get out your house/Get off your block/See something, do something." It's no coincidence that Atlanta's dope markets are known as *the Traps*. So when ATL-based MC T.I. titled his debut release *Trap Music* he was signifying on a level that even he might not have been hip to. The descendants of those early century itinerants now find themselves trapped in urban stasis one hundred years and one Great Migration later. Thus the relationship between blues and hip hop is the relationship between journeys and destinations.

The City is the unnamed protagonist of every hip hop song created. Up out of Hazlehurst and Bessemer, Sumpter, Natchez, Mulberry, and Sanford—two million deep—to lands where you couldn't hear crickets or raise no hogs. In *Philadelphia Negro,* Du Bois fretted, thirty-four years past slavery, that the City would bring black ruination. A century later, Talib Kweli echoed the sage's observation on "Respiration":

> *Look in the sky for God*
> *What you see besides the smog*
> *Is broken dreams*
> *Flying away on the wings of the obscene*
> *Thoughts people put in the air*
> *Places where you could get murdered over a glare*
> *Where everything is fair.*

Hip hop is blues filtered through a century of experience and a thousand miles of asphalt. The City has its own crude dialectics: the mark is to the con as day is to night, the playa is to the lame as east is to west. The City is stone-hewn horizons and temples to vast acquisition. Industrial grit. Vice ecology. Iron arteries. Infinite anonymity and high velocity language. Remixed ritual: malt liquor libation and dice divination. Check out Nas and the cover to his blistering debut *Illmatic.* The image of the rap artist as a young man is superimposed over the legendary Queensbridge Houses—as if he literally has the projects on his mind. The Bridge: the public housing development that cradled Nas and a starting lineup of MCs and producers like MC Shan and Marley Marl. To the MC, shouting out the 'hood, the specific locale and its denizens is a prerequisite. The perspective of the wanderer has given way to the view of the stationary neighborhood rep, one for whom the hood is the universe and the universe is five blocks wide. DJ Quik broke this down with his early-90s assessment that the whole world was "just like Compton." In the blood-feud filled arena of hip hop, where fratricide has become a cliché, a brother has to claim his soil—because who else is gonna preserve one's legend? It would be inconceivable that Mississippi John Hurt would shout down at his Chicago blues counterpart on the basis of geography, but even in the current era of hip hop détente, east is east, west is west, and never shall the listener get that fact twisted.

On another level, the blues relationship to lyricism is distinct from that of hip hop—and most of its pop music descendants. Classic blues were most often collectively authored and speak with the authority of a Negro quorum; hip hop, on the other hand, is obsessed with proprietary concerns. And thus the biter's place of infamy has remained virtually unchanged since hip hop's inception. The biter—a mimic, a knockoff, a counterfeiter of rhyme styles—dwells in the sub-basement of hip hop regard, equaled only by the "rapper" who ain't write his own rhymes. This concern with rhyme larceny and boulevard copyright comes not only as a result of the social and psychological changes in black America since the inception of the blues, but also from a simpler issue: the different instrumentalization of the two musics.

Hip hop has intentionally not produced the equivalent of blues standards like "Stagger Lee" or "C. C. Ryder," because hip hop has no room for "standards" in the traditional sense. The collectively or anonymously authored song in blues is given an individual fingerprint by the artist performing it. And if performance is an ongoing aesthetic experiment, the standard functions as a lyrical or musical constant, the singer's *interpretation* is the variable—along with the nuance of the music backing him. This duality of sameness and difference is fueled by the fact the blues vocalist—who is often also an instrumentalist—controls elements of tempo, chord progression, and detail in the performance of the song, even if the crowd already knows what the lyrics will say. Even as the blues chords are made recognizable by flatted or "blue" notes, the arrangement itself is scarcely redundant. Blues lyrics may change over time, but only in the way that all oral literature is revised according to the failings or embellishments of individual memory. So the blues musician can sing the same lyrics a hundred times while never singing the same song twice.

In the arena of hip hop, the instrumentalist and lyricist are completely distinct; rappers don't spin records, DJs don't rap—and even if they did, no one could excel at both simultaneously. The rapper as an artist owes his existence to the fact that DJs *couldn't* flow verbally while spinning records. On the basic level, a Master of Ceremonies is simply a host; in the beginning, the MC was the entertainer charged with keeping the crowd amped for the *real* performer—the DJ. The earliest of hip hop turn-tablists built their reps by their ability to shoot game over the mic, incite crowd participation, and shout out simple couplets. In short, order, though, DJs like Grand Master Flash, Grand Master Caz, and Kool Herc began outsourcing their rap to hired vocalists, or as they came to be called in the trade, rappers. Flash charted this development precisely:

> I was like totally wack on the mic. I knew that I was not going to be an MC, so I had to find someone able to put a vocal entertainment on top of [my] rearrangement of the music. After so many people tried, the only person that really passed the test—and I think he was one of my lifesavers, with his technique—was Keith Wiggins, who, God rest his soul, has passed. His name was Cowboy. Cowboy found a way to allow me to do my thing and have the people really, really rocking, you know? So we were the perfect combination for some time.

The MC has far less control over what is happening musically than any other vocalist and thus his only resort in creating something new is in the uniqueness of his flow and lyrical content. Otherwise, four rappers reciting the same lyrics over the same track will sound distinct from each other, but qualitatively far more similar to each other than four jazz musicians playing the same arrangement or four blues singers with the same song. *But hip hop does possess a canon of standards:* the instrumentals and beats.

In early hip hop we witness black music stripped down to its most fundamental and ancient elements: vocals and percussion. Early critics of the music—some of them black—disregarded hip hop for its allegedly elementary approach to music, where harmony was often an afterthought. But that kind of perspective missed the point entirely—the sound was elemental, not elementary. And the only thing required for the rapper to break it down was a percussive statement whether it be programmed into an electronic beatbox or improvised by a *human* beatbox. Critics who missed that point found themselves re-mouthing aged platitudes. As Baraka observed in *Blues People:*

> The most apparent survivals of African music in Afro-American music are its rhythms: not only the seeming emphasis in the African music on rhythmic rather than melodic or harmonic qualities, but also the use of polyphonic or contrapuntal effects. Because of this seeming neglect of harmony and melody, Westerners thought the music "primitive." It did not occur to them that Africans might have looked askance at a music as vapid rhythmically as the West's.

Here is the drum—the one instrument expressly forbidden by the antebellum slavocracy—now reinstated as literally the *only* instrument needed for hip hop. Here is the Gospel of Sly Stone: all we need is a drummer. Rappers from time immemorial have been ripping mics to disassembled snippets or instrumentals of "Apache," "Big Beat," "Good Times," or "Impeach the President." George Clinton's "Atomic Dog" has been stripped apart like a six series Benz in the neighborhood chop shop and farmed out to a dozens of would-be producers, but the number of rappers to freestyle over that particular instrumental tilts toward the multiple thousands. In hip hop, the constant is the beat, the variable is both the lyricist's flow and his ability to conjure up a completely different array of themes and punchlines to accompany that beat. Where the singer of blues standards wants to keep the same lyrics as a means of establishing his unique stylings, the rapper wants to do just the opposite—and thus is mandated to eternally dis the biter of rhymes.

In both hip hop and blues we encounter the vocalist as the alter ego of the artist complete with the adoption of a *nom de mic*—the kind of artistic pseudonym that has its roots in the blues tradition. Nobody's mama named their boy Redman, Jay-Z, or Biggie, but neither did anyone come into this world with a tag like Howlin' Wolf, Muddy Waters, or Leadbelly. But there is a distinction even inside this parallel. The two musics have different relationships to the characters they create; the blues musician can sing about evil, but is not necessarily expected to live that way. His use of the first person is as a metaphor for the collective or as a storytelling technique equal to the novel written from the perspective of the protagonist.

Among the zero-sum hustlers of hip hop inc., the credo of "keeping it real" reigns supreme and gives birth to the ever-present contempt for the rapper ain't live it the way he spoke it. "Real" is to the rap industry as "All-Natural" is to fast food supplier, as "New and Improved" is to the ad agency, as "I Solemnly Swear" is to the politician. Witness Jay-Z's assault upon his cross-borough nemesis Nas on "The Takeover":

Nigga, you ain't live it
you witnessed it from your folks' pad
scribbled in your notepad
created your life.

But hip hop's numb insistence upon "reality" misses the fact that the artist's task is to understand and interpret the *whole* world—even those realities that are not his or her own. The demand that there be minimal space between word and deed is ultimately equivalent to demanding that De Niro remain in character as young Don Corleone into the infinite future. Talib Kweli was wise to this angle as well, but few in the mass of MCs were prepared to wrestle with what he put down on "Respiration":

> It's a paradox we call reality
> So keeping it real will make you a casualty
> Of abnormal normality.

But abnormal or not, the rapper, unlike the blues artist, is pressured to adapt (or adopt) his fictive persona in real life. The rapper is judged by a different standard—the ability to live up to his own verbal badness. To get down to the roots, hip hop has come to understand itself in the most literal of terms.

Hip hop is clearly indebted to the blues in terms of its reigning iconography. In hip hop we have the reconstituted trickster—in the absence of the his ironic worldview, or what we might say is the trickster sans *tricksterism*. Even as the music allows room for tricksterish characters like Ol' Dirty Bastard—alias Big Baby Jesus, alias Dirt McGirt—Busta Rhymes, Andre 3000, and Flavor Flav, its perspective is most often materialist and as literal as a fundamentalist. The trickster is secondary in hip hop; in this arena the boulevard 'hood—at least since the inception of Tupac's ghetto ontology "thug life"—has reigned supreme. And the lauded Thug Icon is nothing if not the remix version of the blues' Baaad Nigger archetype. Whereas the Baaad Nigger and the trickster exist as parallel types in the blues, the thug alone has become the patron deity of hip hop: St. Roughneck. Faced with the asphalt bleakness of this world, stripped of the existentialist irony that we see in blues, the result is a perspective that despises weakness, the weak, and everything associated with them.

Whatever else it might be, hip hop is not generally a music of sympathy for the dispossessed. This is a genre that has come to be dominated by a brand of boulevard Darwinism. And on this last point, all distinctions of style, region, and flavor start breaking down. Look close enough at the righteous rage prophets Public Enemy and the Ghericurled gangsta villainy of NWA, circa *Straight Outta Compton*, and what you get is two contrasting images of the same thing: the cult of the Indestructible Nigga. For all their moral indignation and pro-black advocacy, the closest P.E. came to crafting a song sympathetic to the lost and the least was "She Watch Channel Zero"—a moralistic screed about an underachieving soap opera–addicted woman that could've found favor with the Republican National Committee. And in the NWA universe, weakness or loss was a moral felony. The hustler's way is to despise the very addicts he helps to create, and in hip hop the hustler's ethic has come to reign supreme. The damage done by this ethic is widespread, but perhaps nowhere as devastating as in rap's treatment of women. There is, for example, no parallel infamy in popular music to hip hop's so-called *bitch-nigga*—a category that combines the two worst race and gender epithets into a toxic new whole.

> *I got more riches than you*
> *More bitches than you*
> *Only thing I don't got*
> *Is more stitches than you*
> —*Big L*

The above is just one of innumerable such sentiments, issued almost automatically, almost without thought, from the mouths of way too many rappers. This reality is what made songs like Tupac's "Brenda's Got a Baby," Nas' "Black Girl Lost," and De La Soul's "Millie Pulled a Pistol On Santa" truly exceptional. In each case, the artist stepped outside the conventions of hip hop to pen sympathetic narratives about the sexual exploitation of young women.

To reckon with these sad elements is to reckon, by necessity, with the fractured history of black manhood, and the tentatively constructed ideals of black masculinity in America. Out here, on the wasted and wind-blown plains of human conflict, the concept of being both black and a man is and ever was dealt with as a breathing contradiction in terms. And if, for a moment, the Fifteenth Amendment attempted to reconcile that adjective with its noun, the tax on black male suffrage was to be black male life itself. Roughly 3,500 lynchings took place between the passage of the amendment, in 1870, and 1920; the victims were overwhelmingly black men who had been targeted for the South's blood rituals. It was no coincidence that the lynched black body was literally disassembled and distributed to the gleeful white masses—with the penis reserved as the prize token: recreational terrorism.

Georgia, 1899. Sam Hose shrieked at the sight of the knife and quietly urged his tormentors to kill him swiftly. This was plea none was inclined to heed . . . The torture of the victim last almost half an hour. It began when a man stepped forward and very matter-of-factly sliced off his ears. Then several men grabbed Hose's arms and held them forward so his fingers could be severed one by one and shown to the crowd. Finally a blade was passed between his thighs, Hose cried in agony, and a moment later his genitals were held aloft. Three men lifted a large can of kerosene and dumped its contents over Sam Hose's head, and the pyre was set ablaze.

Denial, as the saying goes, is a long river, but it is also the psychological irony that made daily life possible in the buckwild frontier of Racial America. And out of this tendency arises the long tradition of boast, hyperbole, and signifying. What we have is a culture that arising in the context of two centuries of terrorism that habitually, ritually— desperately—rephrases reality, flips the script, and declares the black men indestructible despite all evidence to the contrary. A coping mechanism raised to the level of aesthetic statement. The sages say that a boast is best taken at its opposite face value: the shouted claims of omnipotence, they tell us, serve to highlight one's own fragility. Yet it is equally true that no exploited class of humanity can survive while remaining focused on their own collective impotence.

> *I was born in the backwoods, for a pet I raised a bear*
> *I got two sets of jawbone teeth and an extra layer of hair*
> *When I was three, my crib was a barrel of knives*
> *A rattlesnake bit me and crawled off and died.*
> *—Stagolee, ca. 1896*

> *I tussled with an alligator, rassled with a whale*
> *handcuffed lighting and threw thunder in jail.*
> *I murdered a rock, and hospitalized a brick*
> *I'm so mean I make medicine sick.*
> *—Muhammad Ali, 1963*

Verbal assassin, my architect pleases
When I was twelve, I went to hell for snuffin' Jesus
. . . I melt mics til the sound wave's over
Before stepping to me, you'd better step to Jehovah.
—Nas, 1994

These are lies. But our lies ultimately reveal as much as our truths. And without these lies, it would be impossible to have this specific truth:

Jacksonville, Fla. Jack Trice fought fifteen white men at 3 A.M. on the 12th, killing James Hughes and Edward Sanchez, fatally wounding Henry Daniels and dangerously wounding Albert Bruffum. The battle occurred at Trice's humble home to prevent his 14 year-old son from being "regulated"—brutally beaten and perhaps killed by the whites. On the afternoon of May 11th, Trice's son and the son of Town Marshall Hughes of Palmetto fought, the white boy being badly beaten. Marshall Hughes was greatly enraged and he and 14 other white men went to Trice's house to regulate his little boy. The whites demanded that the boy be sent out. Trice refused and they began firing. Trice returned the fire, his first bullet killing Marshall Hughes. Edward Sanchez tried to burn the house, but was shot through the brain by Trice. Then the whites tried to batter in the door with a log, which resulted in Henry Daniels getting a bullet in the stomach that will kill him. The "regulators" then ran.
—Cleveland *Gazette*, May 30, 1896.

The hope is to make one's claims to bad-motherfuckerdom a self-fulfilling prophecy.

Self-praise, as the maxim tells us, is a half compliment. But on another level, it was insurrectionary for black boys to hail themselves in song and story and right down to names they adopted: *Grand Master* Flash, *Grand Wizard* Theodore, the *Grand Incredible* DJ Scott La Rock. Literal self-aggrandizement. Walter Mosley once pointed out that within the black tradition, heroism is defined simply as survival against great odds—and on another level, the mere *attempt* to survive when one is always outnumbered, always outgunned. The boxer can scarcely afford to admit to his opponent that his unseen shot hurt him all the way down to the chromosomes. Thus: the overblown self-praise that is the corner-

stone of hip hop indicates the scar tissue of black male powerlessness—
and at the same time it testifies to the unrelenting will to survive in the
midst of a deck loaded with wild jokers and stacked way against you.
Call this Stagoleeism.

But hip hop has no room for the antiheroic, no sympathy for the
weak, no blues-like tales of the man lamenting the fact that he sent his
son out to face the regulators. The one who ain't have no choice as he
saw it: surrounded on all sides, no way to protect your boy without
sacrificing your pregnant woman and the two young daughters. Jack
Trice and his boy escaped that night in 1896, but a new mob found his
elderly mother and burned her house to the ground. The lines between
hero and coward, thug and bitch-nigga become blurred when choosing among rival worst-case scenarios. The truth is that some men are
larger than life, but life looms large over very many more. When you
boil away the excess, the hero might just be the coward with a better
plan B.

The two most identifiable American folk heroes are the cowboy and
the gangster, men who conquered the frontiers of sod and concrete, re-
playing the age-old conflict of man versus nature and at the same time,
man versus human nature. In hip hop, so-called Gangsta Rap is an echo
of the folklore tradition of lionizing the outlaw, the robber of banks, and
stealer of men's lives—a tradition that gets its start in black music with
the blues. Within blues and hip hop, the outlaw has a distinct hue—his
crimes are the inevitable product of a system that has made slaves of
human beings and left babies to inherit despair. The bluesman may ask,
"What did I do to get so black and blue?" but that same sentiment is
being echoed by Tupac Shakur's line that "I was given this world/I did-
n't make it."

The critic Robert Warshow has written that the gangster is an American catharsis figure. In a society where official power requires a state-
sponsored public optimism in order to preserve the perception of order,
the gangster's monochromatic world, with its pessimistic symbols and
the inevitably bloody demise of the protagonist, is subversive—in a
way that is most useful to those in power:

> *I watch a gangster flick and cheer for the bad guy*
> *And turn if off before the end because the bad guy dies.*
> —*50 Cent*

In the case of hip hop, the gangster has become the means by which the lives of the marginal, the lesser, the weak have been transformed into entertainment.

It is this gangster ethos that makes gems of sympathetic rendering like Talib Kweli's "Get By" or the Black Eyed Peas' "Where's the Love?" so hard to come by in hip hop. The unanswered question is whether or not hip hop as a genre, as an approach to life, will persuasively deal with human weakness and the ways in which the "weak," the marginalized, and exploited are able to flip the script and instill their lives with meaning. This is the message implicit not only within the musical expression of blues, but also to the blues-contemporary phenomenon of social realism—the aesthetic philosophy underpinning the work of Dos Passos, Steinbeck, and Richard Wright in the 1930s. With *The Grapes of Wrath*, Steinbeck delivered a reckoning with the humanity of heretofore disposable white people. With his murals, Rivera fashioned a vision of the outsized humanity pulsing within the common Mexican laborer. To cut to the quick, what the world needs now is a rapper who can do for the common man and woman verbally what Diego Rivera was able to do with a paint brush and a blank wall.

GROWN FOLK BUSINESS

I pointed out earlier that the "Baaad Nigger" of the blues tradition was reincarnated as the "Real Nigga" of hip hop lore. The blues trickster, on the other hand, descends in hip hop to the playa-pimp, a character who occupies the improvised crossroads of the street corner. He contains the contradiction of male violence while coiffed and primped to the feminine extremes and uses his verbal cunning to literally persuade his stable to do tricks. But the similarity between the two genres on the level of character and archetype does not end with men. Look closely and you find the tradition of the blues woman remixed and replayed in the work of the MC; women whose births were separated by the better part of a century, but who whose work nonetheless bears a family resemblance.

Blues articulated that feeling of running up against the jagged and splintered realities of life, and the specific twists that those realities held for women who were hemmed in by both their race and their gender.

Whether in the boll-weevil stricken soils of the South or the stone and steel depots that the Great Migration had delivered them to, the blues woman spoke of life distilled to the polarities of pain and pleasure, worry, and bravado: The rent note that comes due and the shiftless man with nothing to put toward it. The respite of sexual release and the jealous drive to hold onto what is yours. The major concerns with one's material needs and ones sexuality that find themselves entwined within the music.

The historian Darlene Clark Hine, explained that phenomenon when she wrote women who migrated north and became occasional prostitutes "were extracting value from the only thing society allowed them to sell." Sara Brooks, a black domestic who migrated from Alabama to Cleveland, Ohio, in the 1930s, pointed to this reality when she said that some women "meet a man and if he promises them four or five dollars to go to bed, they's grab it. That's called sellin' your own body, and I wasn't raised like that." But as Hine argued, "As long as they occupied an enforced subordinate position within American society, this 'sellin' your own body,' was, I submit, Rape."

James Baldwin spoke the truth when he said that "Mama has to feed her children and on one level, she really cannot afford to care how she does it." And it was equally true that this self-perpetuating circumstance played into the prevailing ideas that weighed on black women in the first place. The historian Deborah White spoke of that body of myths, sown in the soil of slavery, to justify the sexual exploitation of black women:

> One of the most prevalent images of black women in antebellum America was of a person governed almost entirely by libido, a Jezebel character. In every way, Jezebel was the counter-image of the nineteenth century ideal of the Victorian lady. She did not lead men and children to God; piety was foreign to her. She saw no advantage in prudery, indeed domesticity paled in importance before matters of the flesh.

A loose woman, a sharp-tongue, and a temptress of the type that caused bureaucrats, respectable race folk, and sociologists to wring their hands for an entire century. So it is up against the backdrop of this skewed vision of reality that blues provided women with an arena in which they could articulate life as they saw, experienced, and understood it. The music allowed black women to flip the script and speak of pleasure on their own terms. Such concerns had to be placed in the foreground before Mary Dixon could record a song like "All Around Mama," where the vocalist explains the talents and shortcomings of her past lovers.

> *I met a man, he was a jockey*
> *Did the things he should*
> *Always ready, that's the reason*
> *He could ride so good.*

Dixon could have compared notes with Lil' Kim, whose "How Many Licks?" contrasts the coital skills of men of different races:

> *Had a Puerto Rican Papi, used to be a deacon*
> *But now he be sucking me off on the weekend.*

Blues was the only forum in 1939 in which Ida Cox could've thrown down the gauntlet as she did in "One Hour Mama," a bold-print statement of her sexual prerequisites:

> *I don't want no imitation*
> *My requirements ain't no joke*
> *'cause I've got pure indignation*
> *for a guy what's lost his stroke.*

Lest there be any confusion, the chorus added:

> *I'm a one hour mama*
> *So no one minute papa*
> *Ain't the kind of man for me.*

In Shakespearean terms, there is no new thing beneath the sun; but in this context that observation could be stretched to include between the sheets. "One Minute Man," the 2001 collaboration between Missy Elliott and Trina, expressed a sentiment virtually identical to what Ida Cox had put down sixty-two years earlier.

> *I see you talk a good game and you play hard*
> *But if I put this thing on you, can you stay hard?*
> *If not, you better keep your day job.*

And here the chorus announces in identical fashion:

> *I don't want, I don't need*
> *I can't stand no minute man.*

The poet and blues critic Larry Neal argued that the "disproportionate" concern with the sex act in the blues was a product of commercial influences on the genre—that its discussion of sex grew in direct proportion to the size of the audience willing to pay for that content and record companies' demands for more of the same. That statement explains the hypersexuality that came to be a standard feature of commercially supported female hip hop artists in the mid 1990s. The difference being that within blues, sexuality was generally couched in clever, if thin, metaphors. Hip hop allowed for women to state in unambiguous adjectives the realities of sex. Missy Elliott, for instance, leaves no room for the misconception that she is referring to anything feline when she sings "Pussy Don't Fail Me Now."

Sexually suggestive lyricism was not the level on which blues women and female rappers share a thematic relationship. The earliest critics of hip hop decried the violence associated with the music and articulated with in it lyrics. But hip hop's threats to bodily harm—particularly those issued by women artists—echo the traditions of its ancestor music. The murder of an unfaithful lover is the blues staple. Skip James' threat that

> *If I send for my baby and she don't come*
> *If I send for my baby and she don't come*
> *All the doctors in Wisconsin, they won't help her none*

was not an isolated sentiment. But for every man with a blood grudge against his woman, there was a woman singing:

> *Someone stole my man*
> *So I'm going looking for him*
> *With a .44 in my hand.*

In "Carbolic Acid Blues," recorded in 1928, we witness the common theme of violence between rivals for a man's affections.

I told her I loved her man, grave will be her restin' place
I told her I loved her man, grave will be her restin' place
She looked at me with burnin' eyes, threw carbolic acid in my face.

Those same sentiments were present within hip hop, dating as far back as the 1980s pop confections like Salt-N-Pepa's "I'll Take Your Man." This is not to say that the later artists were derivative or dependent upon blues for material—in most instances, the parallels were unspoken and unplanned. Rather, the point is that hip hop exists as a kindred part of the tradition that also informed the blues and that the women within both genres are, on some level, responding to dynamics that have transcended the years that separate them. The obvious distinction, however, is that female artists were far more widely recognized and influential within the blues than they were in hip hop. Ma Rainey's title of the "Mother of the Blues" may have come into existence as a handle conjured up in the marketing department at Paramount Records, but it wasn't inaccurate. Hip hop, like the Christian Trinity, has bestowed the title of "Father" upon Kool Herc, but there is no mention of the maternal role. That is to say that three decades after its creation, the "Mother of Hip Hop" is a vacant post.

2

The Score

As an MC you will study verbal magic
But watch what you say 'cause you'll attract it
Control the subconscious magnet
From pulling in havoc
"Who am I?"
The MC

Categorizing art is as simple as holding a fist full of water. In hip hop, the standard dichotomies (old school vs. new school, commercial vs. underground, etc.) are as hazy as a Harlem August. As the music through which a new generation announced its aesthetic sensibilities, hip hop is tied to a particular point in history, but even then it is divided into sub-generations of its own. The Benetton-swathed, antiseptically white-Adidas-wearing b-boy who came to the Latin Quarter or Union Square in 1986 to catch Rakim or the Ultra Magnetic MCs, had an experience that was distinct from that of the mock-neck sporting old head who had checked the Treacherous Three at the Disco Fever in 1978. Art respects no borders and time frames, but for our own concerns, hip hop can be divided into four overlapping eras: the Old School, 1974–1983, the Golden Age 1984–1992, the Modern Era, 1992–1997, and the Industrial Era, 1998–2005.

Implicit within each is an approach to the verbal arts that differed from that of both its precedent and successor. The casual observer and the closed-eared critic—of which there are many, if not most—misses the increased artistic complexity that characterized each evolving stage of the music. Where rappers began by stringing together relatively simple rhyming phrases, the art progressed to the employment of metaphor, simile, alliteration, internal rhyme—an entire catalog of techniques to assist in getting one's listening audience open.

•

The irony of history lies in the fact that time moves only forward, but can be best understood by looking backward. It fell to the Old School artists—Grandmasters Flash and Caz, Afrika Bambaataa, Kool Herc, the Cold Crush Brothers, the Crash Crew, the Fantastic Five, Kurtis Blow, the Funky Four Plus One, Sequence, Fearless Four, Spoonie Gee, Busy Bee, the Treacherous Three—to part with the history of weary soul singers and the sequined sync-stepping songsters of the era that preceded them. It fell to them to collectively create hip hop music and see it through its transition from a predominantly live performance medium to its first commercial recordings and distribution.

That transition can't be overestimated; Go-Go music, which germinated from the roots of funk in the 1970s, was, for a variety of reasons, not vigorously pursued by major music industry labels. Consequently, it remained almost exclusively a regional phenomenon, based in Washington, D.C., as well as one that was experienced primarily through live performance. In sharp contrast, the early hip hop recordings that appeared on record labels like Sugar Hill and Enjoy paved the way for the music's expansion from local style to regional sound to national subculture and ultimately global movement. The history of popular music in this country is the history of neglected innovators. It was not in the stars, the cards, or the medium of prognostication of your choosing for these artists to reap the kinds of returns that put them in the CEO tax bracket.

In those earliest days, it might have been harder for the unheralded poet-MC coming of age in the South Bronx and Manhattan to have *not* heard the poetic offerings of the Last Poets, Gil Scott-Heron, or the Watts Prophets. Formed in the aesthetic blast-furnace of the Black Arts Movement, the Last Poets had given new form and elevation to the verbal arts that had come down to them from the traditions of scat syncopation in jazz, the epic folk toasts of the Great Migration era, and the incandescent oratory of Malcolm X. (For the record, with his raspy voice, intellect, and charisma, Malcolm would've made for a serious rapper in another place and time—then again there's just as much argument to be made that he *was* the first great rapper.)

Give "Wake Up, Nigger" from the eponymous debut album a listen and it becomes clear that Last Poets Jalal Nurridin and Umar Bin Hassan are working as proto-rappers, playing many of the verbal techniques that would later become central to the MCs. Their self-titled debut album was released in 1970 and the 1971 follow up *This Is Madness* was released close enough to the beginnings of hip hop to have almost been a contemporary influence. Years later, when Grand Master Flash and the Furious Five's incendiary single "The Message" had infused hip hop with overt political content, Kid Creole would see it as a direct extension of the Last Poets' tradition. "There was nothing in rap like that before except for maybe the Last Poets," he pointed out.

Contrary to popular wisdom, history does not repeat itself—but it is prone to extended paraphrases. Early MCs made use of their aesthetic inheritance in the same way that the generation that created blues had fallen back upon the folklore and musical legacy bequeathed to them by the ancestors who had survived the ordeal of slavery. That said, the irony is that critics and writers generally recognized the influence of the Last Poets more than hip hop artists did themselves. This hazy connection to one's artistic genealogy is not specific to hip hop (try asking the average twenty-three-year-old rock musician about his artistic debt to Ike Turner) but the truth is that an entire generation of hip hop heads were introduced to the Last Poets classic "All Hail to the Late Great Black Man" via Notorious B.I.G.'s first single, "Party & Bullshit," which had sampled a snippet from the track—for decidedly opposite political ends. (This wasn't the last time Big would hijack political anthems for his own boulevardian ends—he famously shackled a segment of Public Enemy's "Shut 'Em Down" to his own "Ten Crack Commandments.") And truth told, the chanted syncopation of Stetsasonic's 1988 release "Freedom or Death," was so deeply indebted to the Last Poets' stylings that the song could've passed as a lost studio session from the revolutionary bards.

A Tribe Called Quest's "Excursions" on *The Low End Theory* featured a rip from the Last Poets' "Time Is Running Out" as the hook. But it was not until Common's 2005 release "The Corner," which featured the Last Poets chanting the hook, did you see major hip hop artists collaborating with their literal elder spokespersons. At the same time, the Last Poets occupied the ironic niche of being the most widely recognized of a whole array of artists who had been mining similar veins. While *The Last Poets* and *This Is Madness* pre-dated the beginnings of hip hop, Gil Scott-Heron's 1974 album *The Revolution Will Not Be Televised* was released as the art form took its first breaths of South Bronx air. Primarily a jazz album, *Revolution*'s claim to the hip hop pantheon was anchored in a title track that found Scott-Heron delivering verse over a hypnotic, funk-indebted bassline—an approach that was so distinct at that point as to warrant classic status. (That same bassline was later lifted and enlisted for Queen Latifah and KRS-One's collaboration "The Evil That Men Do.") At the same time, the other poetic standard-bearers of that era, Amiri Baraka, the Watts Prophets among others, were working toward the creation of another verse form; specifically they sought ever *blacker* forms of self-expression—however that term could be defined.

The debt to that generation of artists was apparent as were the distinctions between the two. In their approach to poetry—maybe as part of their collective efforts to shake themselves free of the constraints of *whiter* poetics—rhyme was often de-emphasized in the work of the Last Poets, Baraka, and Scott-Heron. Hip hop took the elements of verbal expression and percussive accompaniment, but within this new culture rhyme became—and three decades later remained—the most valued element of hip hop lyricism.

It is an irony of history that the complex culture fermenting in the South Bronx and Upper Manhattan came to national attention via the Sugar Hill Gang, an artificially flavored composite group whose "Rapper's Delight" was the first commercially successful recording of the genre. (It was not, however, the first rap record—that distinction belonged to Fatback Band's "King Tim III.") Sugar Hill Records, the indie label owned by Sylvia Robinson, a former R&B vocalist, had gotten in on the ground floor of the movement. That said, they went on to sign future legends Busy Bee, Crash Crew, and Sequence, the first all-female rap act. Rival Enjoy Records, headed by Bobby Robinson, who had discovered Gladys Knight and the Pips, was responsible for the careers of the Funky Four Plus One, Grand Master Flash and the Furious Five, Spoonie Gee, the Disco Four, and the Fearless Four.

Between the 1979 release of "Rapper's Delight" and 1983, the music was perceived as a cute Negro niche market capable of producing free-spirited confections like Kurtis Blow's "The Breaks" in 1980 or the occasional noteworthy musing like Grand Master Flash and the Furious Five's "The Message" in 1982. For the purist, though, the era yielded manifold musical blessings: Afrika Bambaataa's "Jazzy Sensation," "Looking for the Perfect Beat," and the heart-rate spiking "Planet Rock." The Fearless Four released "Rockin' It" and "Problems of the World Today," the Treacherous Three offered "Yes, We Can, Can" and

"Action"—not to mention lesser-hailed contributions from Grand Master Flash and his five MCs like "Scorpio" and "Survival."

To later ears, the toddler awkwardness of the early music is apparent in a way that it never could have been to the contemporary listener. That said, all artistic development begins with shots in the dark and for the artists of hip hop's embryonic stages, there was simply more dark to shoot at. That reality could be seen, for instance, in the awkward intonations and unruly variations in pitch that early MCs employed. Check the Fearless Four's "It's Magic," a classic release whose supernatural boasts made it a thematic cousin to the Tempations' "Can't Get Next to You." The most notable trait of Mike C and Peso's MCing is the wild alternation between false baritone and high-pitched excitement. That brand of unruly intonation had given way to more subtle vocal changes even before the Old School era expired, but their approach to verbal styling wasn't accidental. Just as the rhyme routines of early rappers bore the hallmarks of the soul groups they were imitating, their tonal adventurism was an inheritance from the fast-talking, pitch-varying pseudo-baritone couplets that radio deejays—another ancestor to the hip hop MC—had been practicing for decades.

The radio deejay was in fact a significant precursor to the rapper. That much was clear as early as 1979, when the Fatback Band's "King Tim III (Personality Jock)" appeared. The first recorded rap record featured King Tim throwing down his rap over funked guitar riff. And unlike the Poets, Baraka, or Heron, whose work, in retrospect, sounds raplike, King Tim was *rapping*. The recording is virtually identical in stylistic terms to the early work released by the Furious Five, Grandmaster Caz, and the Funky Four—artists who were the first to be assigned the label "rapper." But the recording is also thoroughly reminiscent of the cadence, intonation, and pitch of the radio entertainers who, by the 1970s, were long-established media personalities.

Rap was delivered to that nebulously defined American deity *the Market* by the Sugar Hill Gang's "Rapper's Delight," but the political birth of hip hop could arguably be traced to Melle Mel's 1982 rhyme manifesto "The Message." While "Rapper's Delight" had remained true to the party spirit at the center of the newborn culture, "The Message" had taken aim at the decaying metropolis—and the decaying lives lived within it—that had made that desperate partying so essential to daily survival in the first place. Frantz Fanon famously pointed out in *Wretched of the Earth* that music and dance remained social safety valves that siphoned anger away and actually made life under inhuman conditions tolerable. Frederick Douglass informed readers of his autobiographical narrative that slavemasters encouraged black people to participate in all manner of recreational diversion in their few moments of respite so as to prevent them from hatching plans to seize their freedom. But with all due respect to Douglass and Fanon, Mel could've schooled them on the revolutionary potential of black joy.

Hip hop was that joy. And on that level, the distinctions between "The Message" and a contemporary party track like the Treacherous Three's "Put the Boogie in Your Body" were less clear than the conventional wisdom would have one believe. "The Message" succeeded—as did Public Enemy's later rhyme polemics like "Welcome to the Terrordome"—primarily because the *form* was blazing. What Melle Mel put down on that record, backed by a cluster of ascending keys and a rotund bassline, was undeniable. Had a lesser MC taken aim at the ills of South Bronx living, no matter how desperately they needed a public exposé, crowds would've ignored it while jamming to apolitical bangers like "Put the Boogie in Your Body." In Melle Mel, though, there was a brilliant combination of both talent and political insight.

Sugar Hill had gotten over with a market success that was, in terms of form, a series of verses strung together without pause. Kurtis Blow's "Christmas Rappin'," released that same year, contained a series of rhymes tied together by the holiday theme. But later offerings more closely adhered to the traditional song structure of sixteen bars followed by an eight-bar chorus. By the time of releases like T-Ski's "Catch the Beat" in 1981, the eight-bar "hook" had become a feature of hip hop songs. Even so, nothing in the music's short history had the kind of resonance of Melle Mel's enduring refrain "It's like a jungle sometimes/It makes me wonder how I keep from going under," which was probably the first classic hook in the art form. His mic skills allowed his indictment of the cancerous ways of Reagan-era America to initiate a genre of *overtly* political hip hop.

Even outside of "The Message" it would be hard to overstate Melle Mel's impact upon the early evolution of the art. (Kool Moe Dee would later point to Mel as the single greatest MC in the history of the music.) In the years, now decades, following the ascent of Grand Master Flash and the Furious Five, there would be dozens of rappers who might be considered to be better than Melle Mel was, but none has been as far ahead of their peers as Mel was circa 1982. His was an unimpeachable position atop the lyricist food chain—a spot he held at least until he ran up against Kool Moe Dee, who had set his sights on Mel's crown after having verbally humiliated Busy Bee. The fact is that for the Melle Mels and Kool Moe Dees there were no precedents; they were artists who had to first create their art form itself before getting down to the business of creating actual art. Every subsequent generation of MCs had a whole genealogy of artists to define themselves against. Melle Mel had a pen, a pad, and an idea.

Run DMC is to hip hop as BC and AD are to history. The emergence of the Queens duo and their insistent opening statement "Sucker MCs" signaled a new era in the music commercially as well as aesthetically. Everything down to their ascetic sartorial choices indicated a shift in priorities. Where Afrika Bambaataa's Soul Sonic Force performed in costumes worthy of George Clinton, Run DMC and Jay opted for the solemnity of all-black outfits offset by black fedoras. Prior to them, hip hop acts blew on stage with Parliament-sized delegations; by the mid-1980s, their format—two MCs and a sole deejay—had become the standard. Not only did the revenues get divided into fewer hands, the structure of their songs changed as well, becoming more individualistic and defined.

But what made the era they inaugurated worthy of the term *golden*—an adjective gleaned from that longest glorified of precious metals in hip hop—was the sheer number of stylistic innovations that came into existence. The era witnessed the emergence of definitive influences, Big Daddy Kane, Queen Latifah, Ice Cube, the Ultra Magnetic MCs, Main Source, 2 Live Crew, Cypress Hill, LL Cool J, MC Lyte, Slick Rick, Too Short, KRS-One, Doug E. Fresh, EPMD, Kool G. Rap, Ice-T, Biz-Markie, NWA, Rakim—almost all of whom were under twenty-one years of age when they made their debuts.

Artists spend years trying to cultivate a unique approach to their chosen form; in these golden years, a critical mass of mic prodigies were literally creating themselves and their art form at the same time. In addition to verbally decapitating MC Shan, for example, KRS-One, the Bronx-born, Jamaica-descended sage and MC, returned hip hop to its Caribbean roots. On tracks like "The P Is Free" on the debut classic *Criminal Minded,* KRS fused bottom-heavy dancehall *riddims* and *patois* seasoned flow with the standards of hip hop articulation. The same would have to be said for Just-Ice, who in addition to pouring the foundation for gangsta rap had blended ragga stylings of his Jamaican ancestry on 1986's *Back to the Old School*. It came as no surprise then that KRS and Just-Ice would find themselves trading island-inflected verses on the 1988's "Suicide."

A Tribe Called Quest constructed an impossibly original sound based on H^2O cool melodic structures that complimented their smoothed-out rhyme patterns. It's hard to believe that their 1990 debut album *People's Instinctive Travels and the Paths of Rhythm* was crafted by artists who were less than two years out of high school. Tribe not only distanced itself even further from the tradition of rhyming routines that sustained the early rap acts, their individual members didn't even necessarily appear on the same songs. On tracks like "8 Million Stories" from *Midnight Marauder* and "Luck of Lucien" from *People's Instinctive Travels*, Phife and Q-Tip delivered distinctive solo lyrical efforts. There had been precedent for this: "The Message," which was released under the name Grandmaster Flash and the Furious Five, featured only Melle Mel rhyming. But that solo performance had underscored rising tensions within the group and factored in their breakup later that year. At the same time as Tribe, De La Soul, their fellow members of the Native Tongues collective, produced *Three Feet High and Rising* which took rhyme to new degrees of abstraction, running extended, elusive metaphors like "Potholes in My Lawn" for the length of an entire song.

The thematic boundaries of what constituted hip hop were not the only thing expanding. Hip hop's relationship to female practitioners of the microphone craft had always been ambivalent at best. And unlike blues, which is literally incomprehensible minus its female articulators; or soul, in which women artists are arguably more aesthetically influential than males; or gospel, where women absolutely are more influential, hip hop's boundary-stretching visionaries were overwhelmingly male. Hip hop's early development had no female artists who were as proportionately influential as Bessie Smith or Aretha Franklin in their respective genres (though, ironically, Sylvia Robinson of Sugar Hill Records was arguably the most important industry executive in the early history of the form). The Golden Era witnessed the ascent of female artists like MC Lyte and Queen Latifah as both artistically and commercially significant, Roxanne Shante as a lyrical assassin with no adjectival modifiers preceding her name, and a regiment of second-tier female MCs like Antoinette, Monie Love, Ice Cream T, and Sparky D. At its core, hip hop was still about a cornered black masculinity using verbs and nouns as a means of defending itself—but the Golden Era brought with it a (grudging) respect for a small collection of women MCs.

From the gate there had been females present within the cipher: the Funky Four Plus One featured Sha-Rock as an equal member of the collective, even if she was designated as the "plus one." As early as 1980, the Sequence had gained note, billing themselves as the first all-female rap group. While their gender had been a marketing point for Sugar Hill Records, the trio of Angie B. (later hailed as the neo-soul songstress Angie Stone), Cheryl the Pearl, and Blondie could not be reduced to a commercial scheme. Releases like "Rapper's Reprise"—shrewdly attached to the label's major hit "Rapper's Delight"—were at least on par with the state of the genre in 1980. (Truth told, Sequence had been preceded by the Mercedes Ladies as the first all-female group, but this historical *sequence* notwithstanding, they were the first commercially recognized women within the genre.) For those growing numbers whose exchanges with the music came via radio and vinyl instead of illegal street jams up in the Bronx, the ladies of Sequence *were* the first female artists. Or might as well have been.

But it was clear that this new era would be different the second the scratchy, high-pitched voice of Roxanne Shante vibrated from a set of speakers in 1984. "Roxanne's Revenge" served as a reprise to "Roxanne, Roxanne," a single released by the admittedly pop rhyme quartet UTFO about an object of their mutual admiration. Shante's reprise lanced their inflated façade, using their own track as backdrop for her lyrical assault. Of the Educated Rapper, who blew onstage garbed in surgical attire, she spat,

> *He ain't that fly and he ain't that great*
> *He don't even know how to operate.*

The reply sold 250,000 copies in the New York area alone, establishing that Shante was not only more lyrically skilled—and attached to a fearsome collective of fellow MCs rooted in the Queensbridge Houses—but also that she came off *harder* than her male nemeses. And that was an unforgivable failing in the male sacred spaces of hip hop. In one of the most un-hip hop moments in known history, UTFO responded by suing the fourteen-year-old Shante for unauthorized use of their track. But Shante's follow-up releases raised concerns that widely undercut the regard in which female artists were held. Relying upon ghostwriters, most notably Big Daddy Kane, for her debut album was incompatible with a genre in which authorship is the measure of one's credibility. In fairness, Kane had supplied lyrics for other artists in the Queens-based MC collective known as the Juice Crew—he ghosted Biz-Markie's comic "Pickin' Boogers." But for male artists, this was still the exception.

Later female acts followed the same business model. Salt-N-Pepa, the first platinum selling female rap act, debuted by lighting into then-reigning male MCs Slick Rick and Doug E. Fresh on "Showstopper," a dis record responding to their classic party cut "The Show." Laced over a simple, programed drumbeat, "Showstopper" was not the commercial success that "Roxanne's Revenge" was, but it did launch the career of the dominant female duo of the era—as well as that of Herbie "Luv Bug" Azor, their producer, manager and lyricist (though on later efforts they assumed a greater degree of creative and lyrical control). In real terms, the duo's commercial significance always outstripped their aesthetic importance. They were firmly on the rapper side of the MC versus Rapper equation. The same could not be said for MC Lyte, who emerged in the late 1980s with a string of now-classic singles—"10% Dis," "Paper Thin," and "I Cram To Understand." In the pantheon of female rhyme slingers, Lyte was the first to gain respect for her standing as a pure lyricist. Equally capable of writing catchy hooks as she was blistering battle rhymes, her 1988 debut *Lyte as a Rock* earned high standing among both the purists and the commercial *overground.* The issue of authorship did not surface in connection with Lyte—she loudly proclaimed ownership of every phrase she dropped over a microphone—but she was not hesitant to raise those same questions about her female peers.

Where commercial artists had come to public attention by tossing lyrical barbs at male counterparts, Lyte's classic battle with her MC nemesis Antoinette provided the first notable crossing of swords between two female artists. On the lethal "Shut the Eff Up," Lyte informed her counterpart that

> *Seeing as you are not wise enough*
> *To do it on your own*
> *The ones who write your rhymes*
> *Might as well hold your microphone.*

Hip hop is and ever was an arena where a loss of avenue credibility is synonymous with a loss of career. Hip hop is perhaps the only musical form where a rival artist literally holds the power to send you to involuntary retirement. In this particular instance, the verbally mediocre Antoinette might have enjoyed a mid-level career had she not run up against Lyte. But the history is what it is and Antoinette was vanquished to the trashbin of disposable MCs by the Brooklynite born as Lana Moorer. Lyte was more of a pure MC than any of her female contemporaries, as evidenced by her skill at both traditional expository rhyming and the deft narrative skills she showcased on cuts like "Cappuccino," where she tells the tale of a woman who gets caught in the crossfire between rival drug dealers on her way to a café and structures the tale such that the victim tells her tale from the afterlife.

Queen Latifah was the nearest of any of her contemporaries to Lyte's standing. Her 1989 debut album *All Hail the Queen* remains important as a period piece, containing on one release the multiple artistic directions—dancehall, hip house, pop—in which the form was moving. Given the dancehall flavorings on *All Hail,* it was not entirely unexpected that KRS-One made a guest appearance on the breakout "The Evil That Men Do," while the hip house release "Come Into My House" showcased her stylistic versatility. While Latifah did not deliver the lyrical sharpness that characterized Lyte's work, she dilated the thematic possibilities of hip hop, ushering in an adamantly and unapologetically pro-sista perspective that had never been more clearly articulated.

At the same time, the outlets responsible for bringing hip hop to the listening public were rapidly being outpaced by younger industry startups. The art form was growing too quickly for any single label to dominate or even represent its full diversity, the way that Sugar Hill and Enjoy had in the first days. By 1987 perhaps Sleeping Bag Records—which had been founded just five years earlier—came closest to representing the breadth of this decade-old genre. The label's roster included Just-Ice, hip hop's ancestral thug and style innovator; Mantronix, the deejay and producer largely responsible for elevating the *electronica* sound that characterized the music during that era; T La Rock, whose classic single "It's Yours" plowed and sowed the stylistic fields that LL Cool J later harvested; EPMD, who were never incendiary lyricists, but whose lethargic, tongue-lazy approach to the microphone helped push the art form even further away from its early styles of enunciation; and

Nice & Smooth, whose deceptively simple flows saved East Coast hip hop from taking itself too seriously.

But given the creative fury of that period, even that roster could not give Sleeping Bag a corner on the market: the same kind of musical trailblazing was going on at Jive (Boogie Down Productions, A Tribe Called Quest), Cold Chillin' (Big Daddy Kane, Kool G. Rap, MC Shan), Tommy Boy (De La Soul, Stetsasonic, Queen Latifah), and, to an even greater degree, Def Jam.

It was during this point that hip hop also came to *sound* different. This golden generation of MCs, who had been in elementary school when they first heard a rhyme laced over a barely dressed drum track, were taking these sparse elements and interpreting them in a thousand ways, each as individual as a fingerprint. But despite their endless differences from one another, they were all confronting the same fact: the music itself was changing. The Sugar Hill Gang had recorded their releases with the backing of the label's house band—just as Motown classics relied upon the staff musicians at the Hitsville, USA studios.

But in 1985 E-mu Systems, a Bay Area–based company that specialized in electronic drum simulators, released the SP12, a new line of machines with a minor addition that would revolutionize the way that hip hop was sonically constructed. The SP12 allowed the user not only to create electronic drum tracks, but also to *sample*, or reproduce previously recorded sounds. A blazing snatch of horn from Maceo Parker or a hypnotic bass line from Larry Graham could now be liberated from their musical contexts, programed into the SP12, and dropped into a pastiche of other collected sounds to constitute an entirely new sound. At its best, the new generation of producers did for music what Romare Beardon's collages had done for art: to take pre-existing scraps of sound or color and compose them into an entirely new piece of art. At its worst, the new production amounted to musical plagiarism.

Either way, the rise of sampling transformed the sonic content of the music from the simple programed bass kicks that had provided the basis for Run DMC's "Sucker MCs" in 1983 into the multi-layered audio collages that backed Kane, KRS, and Rakim just three years later. The live hip hop experience had always been dependent upon the breakbeats and bridges that were constructed by early DJs, but old school recording artists like the Funky Four Plus One had produced their entire body of work using live house bands. Conversely, artists of the Golden Era could produce volumes of work without even *speaking* to a traditional instrumentalist. This added grist to the claims that hip hop was not *art*. But even this was ironic. Sampling placed entire volumes of music on the radar screen for a generation of artists and listeners who might not have otherwise been exposed to it. Stetsasonic was guilty of exaggeration when they wrote "Tell the truth, James Brown was old/'til Eric and Ra came out with 'I Got Soul,'" but they were not entirely off the mark. Sixteen years after they made that observation, the discussion of hip hop's relationship to "art" was still current enough to prompt Talib Kweli to point out that "hip hop artists have more musical knowledge than any generation before us because the nature of hip hop is to sample and loop and build on the past. And the more you get invested in hip hop the more you know about music in general."

The rise of sampling allowed MCs to pair their lyricism with an entire encyclopedia of pre-existing sounds. By the mid 1980s, Stetsasonic, who played their own instruments, could bill itself as *the* hip hop band—indicating that live instrumentalism had become so rare that it could now be the means by which an act was distinguished from the increasingly crowded marketplace of rhyme spitters. A decade later when the Philly-born instrumentalists the Roots released *Do You Want More!???!!?* that same state of affairs existed. Sampling burst on the scene in the mid-1980s, and it has been essential to the genre ever since.

The push to expand the horizons of what was and could be hip hop resulted in manifold new creations. One of these was the fusions of hip house—as seen most boldly in the Jungle Brothers classic "Girl I'll House You" and Queen Latifah's "Come Into My House." Herbie "Luv Bug" Azor stirred together a hip hop/Go-Go cocktail on Salt-N-Pepa's "My Mic Sounds Nice." 2 Live Crew seized the high-tempo electronic sounds that had been the signature of Soul Sonic Force and transformed them into the pavement rattling Miami Bass sound—a style that really hailed the early days of the music in that the MCs lyricism was purely secondary to the intensity that the deejay/producer was putting down.

It should be recalled that the earliest recording efforts of acts like Sugar Hill Gang and the Treacherous Three were backed by studio interpolations of R&B songs. "Rapper's Delight" had been delivered over a musical chassis that had previously supported Chic's "Good Times." Tanya Gardner's "Heartbeat" became the basis for the Treacherous Three's 1981 release "Feel the Heartbeat" and Afrika Bambaataa and the Jazzy 5 had used Gwen McCrae's "Funky Sensation" to undergird their single "Jazzy Sensation" that same year.

This had already begun to change by the time Grandmaster Flash and the Furious Five took to employing funk-disco inspired scaffolding to support bangers like "White Lines." Early 80s releases like "Planet Rock" and jazz trumpeter's Herbie Hancock's hip hop opus "Rock It" diverged from the R&B mold in favor of hyper-tempo techno pulses and digital effects (a style that died on the vine as far as East Coast hip hop was concerned, but was reincarnated in the Miami Bass sound). If it wasn't apparent earlier, the door was slammed on the previous era by the insanely kinetic banger "Ego Trippin'" released by the Ultra Magnetic MCs in 1986. Defined by a disassembled scrap of keyboard, an endorphin-spiking digital scream hijacked from James Brown and an insistently whispered chorus—all layered over a Funky Drummer-esque percussion line—"Ego Trippin'" was so radically different as to be almost frightening. Add to that the stream-of-consciousness abstraction of MCs Kool Keith and Ced Gee and you wound up with one of the least acknowledged but widely influential singles of the entire era. Keith, who would later reincarnate himself as Rhythm X, Dr. Octagon, and Black Elvis, threw ethereal, nearly nonsensical verses in a high-pitched voice that contrasted Ced's choppy, staccato flow. Blasphemously, Ced didn't even bother to *rhyme* his verses on the track. The sound anticipated the aural anarchy that Hank Shocklee would commission for Public Enemy and the feeding frenzy that would quickly make James Brown the most sampled musician in the history of hip hop. Such was the state of affairs that KRS-One would later declare James Brown to be the first true hip hopper. (This was a claim that had even more weight if you considered the family resemblance between JB's anti-drug opus "King Heroin" and the syncopated poetry of early hip hop.)

> *Hip hop pioneers we didn't ask to be*
> *But right then hip hop changed drastically*
> *People didn't want to hear the old sound*
> *We started sampling beats from James Brown.*
> —KRS-One, "Outta Here"

The Ultra Magnetic's debut release *Critical Beatdown* was heavily indebted to Soul Brother Number One, even on the level of song title: "Give the Drummer Some," "Ain't It Good to You," and "Watch Me Now" were the most easily identified Brown influences, but by no means the only ones. Ced Gee's friend and sometime collaborator, the legendary late Paul C., had similarly jacked JB for the basis of Supa Lover Cee and Casanova Rud's club hit fittingly titled "Do the James Brown." The Ultras developed their idiosyncratic approach to production and lyricism on a string of singles, including "Funky," an elliptical, off-kilter track based on a descendant two-note piano that later became the basis for Tupac and Dr. Dre's "California Love." (Ced Gee, the Ultra Magnetic's main producer later turned this track inside out and laid it down in support of KRS-One's classic "The Bridge Is Over.") In short order, the technology transformed used record bins into aural scrap yards, and that long-neglected album collection gathering dust into the attic into a vinyl encyclopedia of sounds.

The reliance upon sampling marked increasing disjuncture between hip hop and R&B on the level of sound. The programed drumrolls, repetitive effects, overlaid scratches, and stuttered catch phrases that would eventually become sonic clichés of hip hop production owed their existence to the new musical technology. R&B, even at its sappiest 1980s incarnations, still sounded *musical.* The emerging sound of hip hop managed to be both elemental and technological simultaneously. And because one could now become a major producer without knowing how to read music, hip hop's status as an aesthetic stepchild was further solidified. To be accurate, though, by the 1980s R&B was a wasteland headlining artists for whom blackness was incidental. As the music critic Nelson George pointed out, assimilation and racial neutrality were the order of the day as artists like Michael Jackson, Prince, and even former Commodore Lionel Richie cultivated personas that were only vaguely black but wholly marketable.

Whatever else it was or was not, hip hop remained unapologetic and, like punk rock, was too busy aggressively articulating itself to be concerned with meeting someone else's standard of art. Still, there was not absolute musical apartheid between R&B and the emerging hip hop genre; Chaka Khan's 1984 single "I Feel for You" famously included a rap intro from Melle Mel and Jody Watley enlisted the rhyme skills of none other than Rakim for an interlude on 1989's "Friends." In short order, the rap bridge became a standard part of the R&B song structure. And beyond the transformation in terms of sound, the expanding reach of the music brought new thematic concerns.

The 'hood, and by this I mean not the generic graffitied walls and high-crime zones of the suburban imagination, but the specific locale, streets with particular names and stories, the individual terrain that gave birth to an individual artist had always been at the center of hip hop. But because the music was rapidly going national, those specific, local communities came to carry additional significance. Run DMC inaugurated and ended their reign demanding recognition of "Hollis Ave.," LL claimed his native Farmer's Boulevard with the zeal of a proselytizing missionary, and NWA willfully titled their debut *Straight Outta Compton*.

For the bulk of this time, the East Coast—hip hop could now be divided into coasts—held artistic dominance. Better yet, the East Coast (really New York, Jersey, and a sprinkling of Philly reps) had progressed past their Old School into another epoch while other locales were still in the midst of their own embryonic Old Schools. For the South and West, MCs like Shy-D and Ice-T were the Melle Mel and Kool Moe Dee of the day. A handful of acts like NWA were exceptional, though. Headed by the flow-impaired Eazy E and relying heavily upon Dr. Dre's production skills and the ghosting talents of Ice Cube, the group's most notable MC, the collective was more interested in issuing credible threats and verbal muscularity than in constructing intricate rhyme patterns.

The MCs of the West Coast were generally looked down upon by their eastern counterparts; their tendency toward languid, head-throbbing cadence was taken as the absence of lyrical ability. Bear in mind, Easterners were overstuffing their bars with syllables, labyrinths of alliterations, and clever verbal effects to illustrate their dexterity of tongue. (A classic Big Daddy Kane during this point announced that "I could sneeze sniffle or cough/e-e-even if I stutter, I'ma still come off.")

That credible-threat angle wasn't virgin terrain: Just-Ice, the neglected and literally felonious father of gangster rap had worked this same formula two years earlier with his 1986 solo release *Back to the Old School* (it has to be recognized that the concept of Old School has been relative—just two years into the Run DMC era, Just-Ice was lamenting for hip hop's bygone early days) and Schoolly D's casually malignant "PSK" (1987) fit the same mold. The under-recognized innovation of NWA, though, lay in their early reliance upon the West Coast funk tradition that gave even their early efforts a degree of melodic fullness and depth that East Coast producers would not match until much later. In that same vein, New York–based disco had provided the aesthetic underpinnings of early East Coast rap to such an extent that at hip hop's outset some used the terms *disco* and *rap* interchangeably and certified rap acts went by handles like the Disco 4. Similarly, the evolving Southern hip hop scene made use of its regional roots in soul music in carving out its signature sounds.

In the Cali context, Dr. Dre's 1992 solo debut *The Chronic* was sonically (and thematically) distinct enough to effectively usher in a new era in the music. But even before that episode had unfolded, Dre-produced releases like NWA's *Efil4zaggin* (1989) (Niggaz4Life spelled backward) spoke the truth about Cali's musical complexity outstripping that of East Coast hip hop, which was then centered around permutations of 808 claps and hijacked samples of earlier sounds. Not coincidentally, Dre was also a musician whose ability to play the keys set him apart from the vast majority of his East Coast counterparts (and many of his West Coast ones as well). In creating Public Enemy's trademark sound of layered, anarchic, anti-harmonic noise, producer Hank Shocklee had picked up where the aural disorder of cuts like the Ultra Magnetic MCs "Ego Trippin" had left off. But even with that in mind, the disparity was clear and likely the product not so much of hip hop itself. The older disparity between the musicianship of disco and funk provided the musical base for East and West Coast rap respectively. At the very least, Dre's abilities as a keyboardist had as many commercial implications as artistic ones: a riff from Sly Stone, for instance, that had been interpolated by musicians would be far cheaper to license than an actual sample from the record on which it appeared, which could require the consent of record labels, artists, and however many entities had stakes in the song's publishing rights.

Ice Cube's 1990 EP *Kill at Will* and his follow-up solo release *Amerikkka's Most Wanted* marked the first time a Cali artist had successfully breached the coastal divide. That accomplishment was the product of the shrewd partnering of Cube's stark, South Centralized tales from the 'hood with the endorphin-releasing sonic madness of the Bomb Squad production team that had shaped Public Enemy's sound. Wedding his copywritten South Cali flow and asphalt reportage to the noise architecture of the Bomb created a hybrid, bi-coastal sound that elevated the genre above its petty East-West sectionalism. It was, to cop the term wrongfully applied to the collaboration of Jay-Z and R. Kelly, the best of both worlds.

The wake of *Amerikkka's Most Wanted* and the follow-up *Death Certificate* saw Ice Cube hailed as a foul-mouthed wiseman who predicted the 1992 L.A. riot months before it actually went down. Beyond his claims to ghetto clairvoyance, Cube is counted among that blessed number of artists to survive more than a decade in a field where patricide is considered an art form. The body of work that he produced between *Amerikkka's Most Wanted* and *The Predator* in 1993 established him as Stagolee's response to urban decline. It confirmed him as Bigger Thomas, reincarnated and equipped with a 12-gauge scowl and a record deal. And way before Notorious B.I.G. or Tupac went public with their existential angst, Cube's elegiac "Dead Homiez" poured a metaphorical libation for the young, black, and departed. Quiet as it's kept, Cube was the earliest of the Cali verbalizers to demand—and receive—his due respect from hip hop's East Coast establishment.

He later shared that distinction with his fellow Californians Cypress Hill. Of their first release, the critic and hip hop historian Jeff Chang wrote:

> But this self-titled debut—the second inspired West Coast answer to BDP's *Criminal Minded* and a Spanglish response to the first, NWA's *Straight Outta Compton*—brimmed with importance. If it didn't claim knowledge, it offered street wisdom.

In an arena in which allegiance to the get-high was nearly ubiquitous, Cypress managed to move to the front of the weed line to become the most prominent exhorters of the smoke. While rap philistines shouted the virtues of the chronic, Cypress moved to create an actual marijuana aesthetic. Their eponymous debut set the mold: the collective favored dark, dense sounds that bubbled up from the haunted corners of the psyche. In his production work within the trio, Muggs created a style of music as individual as a DNA fingerprint. The beats warbled up from the bottom of the register and consistently sounded like a bass drum being played at the bottom of the San Francisco Bay. This was music to get stoned by. In the Cypress Hillian world, time moved like an old 45 being played at 33 rpm. The unstated goal of their sound was to produce an audio contact high, to have the listener look at the world through newly bloodshot eyes.

The unstated element of Cypress Hill's significance was their background as Latino artists. From day one, the culture had been created by a dynamic interaction between African American youth and young people descending from the English- and Spanish-speaking Caribbean. Charley Chase of the Cold Crush Brothers, Tito of the Fearless Four, and

Ruby Dee of the Fantastic Five were all Latino, as were a significant por-
tion of the groundbreaking artists in other hip hop forms—the short list
would include the breakdancer Crazy Legs, the graffiti artist Futura,
and Pink. Over the course of the 1980s, however, hip hop came to be
seen as dominantly, if not exclusively, African American; Latino rappers
were seen as niche market novelties.

Cypress existed outside those constricting categories, gathering a
wider audience than other Latin rap contemporaries like Mellow Man
Ace or Kid Frost. In classic context, B-Real contrasted the inebriated
drawl of background sounds with his own nasal drone. On tracks like
Black Sunday's "I Wanna Get High," the lead vocalist wails like a kid lost
in the mall, supported by tracks diabolical enough to justify exorcism.
Taking aim at his political antagonists, he spoke: "My oven's on high
when I smoke the Quayle/Tell Bill Clinton to go and inhale." Sen Dog
was content to play the heavy, growling out the chorus from the outer
precincts of the studio, occasionally piping in a menacing verse of his
own. Right down to the cover art, C.H. was responsibly for the first
identifiably gothic approach to the art form.

For the underground purists, Kool G. Rap merits mention in the
same sentence, albeit a few commas down, from Old School legends
Rakim, Big Daddy Kane, and KRS-One. Heroically overcoming a
speech impairment to wrap his tongue around some of the most complex syllables this side of a Mandarin tongue-twister, the Kool Genius
of Rap opened doors for later lispers like EPMD's Erick Sermon and a
whole rack of other hip hop non-enunciators. (Most rappers claim to
"spit" lyrics. The G. took that term literally.) No question, G. Rap threw
down a musical gauntlet with 1987's "It's a Demo" and the B-side, "I'm
Fly." The bard came off with the standard repertoire of conspicuous
consumption and resumé-flashing, but kicked it with a wit and off-kilter use of vocab that put him ahead of the pack. G. Rap, along with
Just-Ice, pioneered the subgenre that came to be known as "gangsta
rap," but unlike his artistic progeny, G. relied more upon verbal creativity than shock value to get over. Plus, G. Rap played viceroy to the
dynasty of South Queens rappers who treated the rest of hip hop the
way the New York Yankees perpetually treat the American League
East.

Whatever the case, G.'s tales from the stark side eventually
dropped the verbal ingenuity that gave them their flair and started traf-
ficking in Ice Cubean realism. The higher body counts and fewer deft

similes had heads disbelieving that this was the same verbalist who said, "Talk about a battle/but you ain't yet ready for war/your metaphor sucks/more than a whore." Ergo, G. Rap's sole notable offering of the era was the hitman's eye narration of "Ill Street Blues."

The inconsistency that defined G. Rap's career was contrasted by the consecutive brilliant releases of his rhyme contemporary, Guru of Gangstarr. In that sweet margin of time before the demise of the radical self-righteousness of Public Enemy and the reign of nihilism-chic à la NWA, Gangstarr virtually ruled the fleeting niche of thug-wiseman. Way before Tupac Shakur became the avatar of Avenue Wisdom, Guru was working on a slick lyrical fusion of the boulevard (i.e., gang) and the ethereal (star). There was no telling where Guru might go with his flow. In his rhyme book the profane street parable (hip hop's version of a standard) was held in equal reverence to the profound Surah. Asphalt metaphysics.

Plus, the ranks were deep. Listen, Guru, and the crew he ran with— the ad-hoc collection of MCs surrounding the aptly titled DJ Premier— rolled thick, like a host of ghetto potentates with diplomatic immunity. This despite the fact that Jeru the Damaja was the only member of the extended family to make any real noise. Still, the twisted, asymmetrical loop Primo hooked up for Jeru's "Come Clean" warrants a spot right next to the malevolent funk Dr. Dre crafted for "187" and RZA's early Wu-Tang efforts in the sonic archive of 90s hip hop production.

Backed by Premier-orchestrated beats that were dense enough to make lead float, Gangstarr's opening efforts on *Step in the Arena* hinted at what was to come. By the time they followed up with *Daily Operation,* their standing within the art form was beyond impeachment. Before the decade was out, Guru had gone diasporan, recruiting French rapper MC Solaar and releasing "Jazzmatazz"—the deft mélange of hip hop and jazz that stood head and shoulders above the feeble preceding efforts at blending the two genres. And herein lies Guru's significance to the form. Guru was literally miles ahead of his MC peers who *spoke* of a wider black world—he alone was in artistic dialogue with that world.

Guru was never a pyrotechnic MC delivering fireburst punch lines; his flow at points offered as much inflection and variation as a dial tone. But like the best musicians, he played to his weaknesses, turning his smoky baritone and deadpan delivery into stylistic hallmarks. He put that same form to good effect on "The Ownerz"—Gangstarr's late-career release, delivered twelve years after *Step in the Arena.* Over the rotund bass loop of the initial track, "Put Up or Shut Up," Guru spits that "you know it's time to sit and think/before we hit the brink/locker room at a prizefight before we hit the ring." Augmented by a minimal snare and cymbals, the cut is a wonder of simplicity.

But the dominant element of that era was, without question, Public Enemy. Their ascent marked the first time since "The Message" that the music's foremost artistic trailblazer was also its most politically inclined. The political fervor of their sophomore release *It Takes a Nation of Millions to Hold Us Back* came across like an unseen overhand considering the comparatively innocuous political jabs issued on their 1986 debut, *Yo, Bumrush the Show*. While their political significance has been widely recognized, PE's artistic significance was second only to Run DMC's in that era. Lead lyricist Chuck D literally shouted lyrics over background tracks that were deliberately mixed in too high. The lyrics themselves were politically charged double entendres—as if an MC had returned to the tradition of the Negro spirituals that slaves encoded with messages of subversion.

Their singular genius lay in the fact that they recognized rap music as a form of media at a time when the most astute practitioners of the genre (e.g., EPMD) were just getting hip to the idea of music as business. In that regard—and several others—PE was way ahead of the curve, expanding the functions of their art form. They enlisted their own "media assassin," Harry Allen. They conjured up an analogy about the music being a black CNN, set out to transform rap into straight-up network, beaming survival notes to all of us trapped in the synapses of society. Talking drums banished from plantations were now digitally resurrected and transmitting worldwide. Their emergence marked the beginning of a whole new subgenre. But the hook wasn't their politics so much as the raw noisiness of their aesthetic. Lead lyricist Chuck D's vocal boom was the perfect counterpart to the random bits of discarded sound—audiotrash—that the Bomb Squad ironed into music. This was screed poetry and Chuck D was probably the only rapper capable of turning that assessment into an asset. He did not so much rhyme as he exhorted. He had copped a lesson from his Black Arts Movement precursors and learned how to elevate a rant into a tour-de-force. It was the perfect wedding of dissonance and dissidence.

At first glance, the ensemble looked like the supreme example of niche marketing. Here was a psuedomilitia clad in army surplus fatigues, toting plastic Uzis and led by two clichés of Black existence—the humorless militant and the unreformed coon, aptly played by Chuck D and the clock-wearing lyrical sideman Flavor Flav. But PE was somehow more than the sum of its constituent parts, more than just overworn stencils shaded in by the Def Jam marketing department. Their success is owed to the fact that cliché or not, Chuck became one of the most articulate voices of the era and Flav was the comic relief that made him tolerable.

That reality became clear in late 1986 when the group conducted an "audio tour" through *Yo, Bumrush the Show* on an underground college hip hop station broadcast from their native Long Island. Chuck broke down the significance of "Miuzi weighs a ton" and a cut that had heretofore been considered standard hip hop hyperbole exploded into a metaphoric assault on the state. The next year *Nation* raged out of the Strong Island to "reach the bourgeois/and rock the boulevard," spouting undiluted black nationalism. "Night of the Living Baseheads" was one of the few anti-drug rap songs that didn't come off like a public service announcement. But the real magnum opus was couched between a hijacked snippet of a Jesse Jackson speech and a James Brown track. The fanatic sirens and whistles and Chuck's vocal saturation bombing on "Rebel without a Pause" seared the single onto playlists and etched *Nation* into the pantheon of greatest hip hop albums ever made. The shouted introductory "Yes, the rhythm, the rebel" rested among the most distinguishable opening lines in the genre. While the specifics of their aesthetic were inimitable, PE's rhyme radicalism filtered over into dozens of artists of that era, influencing a diverse array of acts like Paris, X-Clan, and the Coup and clearing the way for the more political releases of Boogie Down Productions like 1988's *By All Means Necessary*, 1989's *Ghetto Music*, and *Edutainment* the following year.

Like the aesthetic transitions of jazz in the post–World War II era, hip hop in its golden era evolved in dialogue with its times. It was no coincidence that its most politicized offerings came in the midst of the so-titled Reagan Revolution. It was in the years between 1983 and 1992 that the music evolved into a mature art form with regional sub-flavors. That development would—antagonistically and tragically—be a dominant theme in the era that followed it.

Listen to Dr. Dre's *The Chronic* now, whenever your *now* happens to be, and its musical significance is likely to be lost on you. And that fact ironically highlights how extreme its significance really was. The trademark distinctions that made the 1992 release a breaking point in the history of hip hop and ushered in the music's "modern era" have now become so widely accepted as to be commonplace elements. Released in the immediate wake of the LA rebellion, *The Chronic* marked another uprising, albeit one in which the fires were metaphorical and the firing was lyrical—at least most of the time. In the wake of NWA's dissolution, Dr. Dre, who had been the group's sonic architect, fell back upon the ancestral funk and carved out a basis for not only a gangster rap but a gangster *sound* to wed it to. Though it was released under Dre's name, the album was actually an anthology of artists on the newly established Death Row Records label. The laid-back post-smoke tempo of the album stood in stark contrast to the frenetic, deliberately noisy aesthetic that accompanied Public Enemy, who had previously held the most recognizable approach to sound in the music. On the level of sound, Chuck D theorized that the Cali production was constructed with car stereos in mind in contrast to the East Coast where the primary listening device was still the Walkman and headphones. Whether this held water or not, the regional styles did seem to reflect the stereotypes of laid back West Coasters and the fast-talking, quick-paced New Yorkers. And where Chuck D and his host of political acolytes and comrades had crammed meaning into polemic verses, *The Chronic* marked the ascent of not only the West Coast and Death Row, but also of gleefully G'ed out style that glorified the lumpen hustlers of the 'hood in ways that only Melvin van Peebles and Huey P. Newton could truly appreciate.

When the story gets told correctly, later East Coast acts like Mobb Deep and Noriega, who came up through the hallowed proving grounds of the Queensbridge Houses and mined the curb-level grit of the City for material, might be in deeper aesthetic debt to Dre's West Coast ensemble than they are to the MC tradition of their home asphalt.

Snoop's trademark drawled-out Mississippi-derived syllables and the tortured-soul poetics that Tupac Shakur voiced on *All Eyez on Me* and *Me against the World* pushed the art form in new directions that became innovations lost on the once-supreme East Coast artists. The burgeoning inter-coastal rivalry gave added weight and expectations on the East Coast's benchmark contributions of era, Notorious B.I.G.'s blistering *Ready to Die*, Nas's *Illmatic*, and the installment plan of Wu-Tang Clan releases beginning with *Enter the Wu-Tang (36 Chambers)* through Raekwon's *Built Only for Cuban Linx* and GZA's under-heralded *Liquid Swords*.

The ascendancy of the West Coast at this point was akin to an upset victory for the purists who had long associated the East Coast with the forefront of the art form. (In the mid-1980s, the Easterners were so self-assured that an important, if under-recognized artist like Mikey D could refer to his crew as the LA Posse—referring to the Laurelton section of Queens, New York—and be assured that no one would possibly confuse the reference for the City of Angels.) But there were roots on the West that had been germinating throughout the 1980s, providing a basis for the new era. Importantly, Ice-T's 1987 *Rhyme Pays* had marked a jumping off point for the West in the same way that KRS-One's *Criminal Minded*—released the same year—had laid down a standard for the East. Ice-T, while associated with the new school of LA-based artists, was a few years older than most of his peers (*Rhyme Pays* was released when he was twenty-eight) and in an art form as new as hip hop, those few years made a substantial difference. His lineage in the flow ran deeper. That is to say that Ice-T's points of hip hop reference were Bambaataa and Flash—not Run DMC and Whodini.

The album's centerpiece, "6 in the Mornin'," has been aptly compared to Schoolly D's notorious "PSK" as a touchstone for the evolving gangster theme in the music (and despite his later incarnations as hip hop's resident metaphysician, KRS-One's *Criminal Minded* was part of that same ethos). Ice-T derived his nom de mic from Iceberg Slim, the legendary pimp-novelist who had provided the world with street lit gems like *Trick Baby* and *Mama Black Widow* and remained indebted to the elder Ice for his thematic content and perspective. On the strength of *Rhyme Pays* and the later *Power*—which was as recognized for the cover art featuring Ice-T's scantily clad wife as it was for its musical content—Ice became the primary articulator of LA's street parables and the characters who inhabited them. Where Run DMC's rap-rock collaborations like "Walk This Way" and "King of Rock" came off as well-executed marketing schemes, Ice-T's selection of musical elements—as likely to feature heavy metal rips as James Brown riffs—dated him as a product of the Bambaataa-era when the art form was truly eclectic in its musical tastes.

Similarly, Too Short, another of the West's founding artists, had relied upon the subject matter of 70s black pulp for his own lyrical content. His 1989 *Born to Mack* was released on the East Coast Jive label, but his status as a commercially viable artist had been solidified through his two independently released albums as well as his Bay Area years of literally selling his material from his car trunk. *Rhyme Pays* and *Born to Mack* were identifiably West Coast records on the level of music and, particularly in the case of Too Short, lyricism. The plodding cadences of his noted "Freaky Tales"—a wild and wildly misogynistic ride through the alleged sexual exploits of the rapper—were sharply contrasted by the increasing rhyme density of his Eastern counterparts.

Gangsta—as the media termed the dawning movement inside the form—was to become a dominant theme within the music and provide hip hop with its most brilliant if retrograde and controversial content. It was this subform that would be responsible for expanding the ranks of hip hop critics from those knowledgeable about the art form to the upper echelons of American politics—and individuals who had not studied rhyme since nursery school. Still it is possible to overplay the G card—as is often the case, especially when dealing with West Coast hip hop during the era. Gangsta's bold, eighteen-point-font headlines overshadowed developments that were of at least equal aesthetic importance that were taking root on the West Coast as well.

In five consecutive years—1990 through 1994—West Coast artists produced seminal releases and introduced new voices that were as idiosyncratic, original, and creative as the best work to emerge in the mid-1980s. Beginning with Digital Underground's 1990 *Sex Packets* and culminating in Casual's *Fear Itself* in 1994, the "alternative" rap of the West Coast provided an important counterpoint to the perspectives of grit dealers like Cube or MC Eiht. Though inhabiting the same geography, DU's perspective could not be confused with that of Bay Area pioneers like Too Short and Spice 1. The ironic footnote is that it was the sex-comic Digital Underground—Shock G. (and comic alter-ego Humpty Hump) and Money B.—who were responsible for giving the thug immortal Tupac Shakur his entrée into the music industry.

The seeds of a California underground scene were further cultivated by the appearance of Del Tha Funky Homosapien's *I Wish My Brother George Was Here* in 1991. Del, who was, ironically enough, a cousin of the Gangsta king Ice Cube. Both were groundbreaking West Coast lyricists but that's where the family resemblance ended. Del's work was often abstract to the point of puzzlement and characterized by witty meandering on mundane problems like public transportation ("The Wacky World of Rapid Transit") and freeloading friends ("Sleepin on My Couch"). Importantly, Del was served as the advance guard for the Hieroglyphics, the collective that also included Souls of Mischief and Casual.

Swimming against the prevailing tide of P-Funk samples, Souls constructed a breezy, laid back style relying heavily upon jazz horns to support their clever lyricism. With a handful of exceptions, the artists further to the south had largely sacrificed wit for vividly violent narration—the unspoken creed being that real gangstas practice gunplay, not wordplay. In contrast, Tajai of Souls delivered clever puns like "I flip the script like a dyslexic actor." The distinctions went all the way down to titles: where vintage Ice Cube titled his EP *Kill at Will*, Souls of Mischief supplied content like the bohemian "Live and Let Live." There was a facile temptation to see the Hieroglyphics as the West Coast corollaries of the Native Tongues, but that comparison ended with a common tendency toward jazz riffs and lyrical abstraction. The Souls in particular were edgier, harder, and deliberately overlapped their lyrics in such a way as to recall the ancients like the Fearless Four and the Crash Crew. (With four lyricists, A+, Phesto, Tajai, and Opio, they *could* channel the older larger groups—something for which the two-man rap groups of the era were understaffed.) Years later, the breezy and beautiful title track for their release *93 'Til Infinity*—a fertile blend of deft lyricism and floating xylophone notes—remains a concise statement on that entire era.

The evolving scene was not solely a North Cali phenomenon. A year prior to *93*, Pharcyde's debut, *Bizarre Ride to the Pharcyde*—truth in advertising if there ever was any—had been released. Characterized by melodic flows that bordered upon scat rhythms and day-in-the-life-of-a-slacker content, Pharcyde was probably the most thoroughly conceived and flawlessly executed of any of the alternative releases of that era. Pharcyde, Souls, and Del shared a common trait beyond the appellation of "alternative"—a sense of humor. On Pharcyde tracks like "Quinton's on His Way" and "If I Were President," the group delivered clever lyricism and witty parenthetical observations that were literally comic relief considering the asphalt grimness of other segments of the music.

Taken as a whole, they constituted a dissident movement against the nascent G-themed music that was quickly becoming the industry standard. The fact that the troublesome label "alternative rap" could be plastered onto the diverse array of lyricists who found interest in subjects beyond underclass crime drama was in itself indicative of what "mainstream" hip hop had become. Acts like Souls and Pharcyde had *alternative* kin in East Coast groups like Lords of the Underground and Das Efx that were almost equally quirky and gleefully out of step with the bitches and bullets crowd. By the early 90s, the art took itself so seriously that it almost demanded the gang satire that Black Sheep provided on 1994's *A Wolf in Sheep's Clothing* and Masta Ace's concept album *Slaughtahouse*. East Coast artist OC dissected the trend on the masterful "Time's Up" in 1993 lamenting the state of affairs as:

> *Non-conceptual, non-exceptional*
> *Everybody's either crime-related or sexual*

While the pens of critics and observers in national publications rightfully hailed the supremacy of the West Coast artists, it has to be recalled that it was a victory, not a shutout. To be precise, Wu-Tang Clan, the nine-member ensemble of MCs hailing from the forgotten precincts of Staten Island and referring to themselves in obscure martial arts metaphors, were aesthetic originals. Distinguishing themselves from the disposable icons, momentary it-men, and weeded-out bards of the boulevard that were being mass produced by labels on both coasts, Wu-Tang represented a definably distinct approach to the art form. In an age of glory-struck soloists, the Wu-Tang ensemble mastered the art of the collective. And while their contemporaries spat variations on the same genital-material themes, deciphering Wu-Tang was about as simple as reading Braille hieroglyphics.

Wu-Tang Clan harked back to the long-past days of Parliament-Funkadelic, becoming the first hip hop group to construct an extended metaphor that defined their entire body of work. We're not speaking about Parliament's universe in which funk and funklessness are stand-ins for good and evil, but whole cosmology wrung from comic books and Saturday afternoon kung fu flicks. Thus, the Wu-Tang home province of Staten Island is reborn as Shao-Lin. Their verbal acuity is referenced as the sharpness of the sword and their aural signature includes clacks thumps and whizzes jacked from classics like *Enter the Dragon*. These were MCs on a mission so deep that even their aliases had pseudonyms: Method Man aka Johnny Blaze; Ghostface Killah aka Tony Starks (which also happens to be the true identity of Iron Man, another of his identities). And like the galactic funk engineers of Parliament, Wu-Tang's chief visionary RZA conceived of a band as a community employment program. Prior to their emergence, a black musical act had not blown onstage with as many people as Wu-Tang since the Carter Administration. But the similarities ended there. Unlike the funksters of yore, Wu-Tang was all about grit, grime, and slum parables.

In the wasteland of corporate music, there's a fine line between vision and shtick. And true indeed, a lesser squad of verbalists would've found themselves interred in the graveyard for wack ideas. But such was not the case. Wu-Tang's self-described "first branch" was nine-men deep with a whole roster of Staten Island progeny waiting to get put on. The combination of RZA's liquid, noir production style and the ability of wordsmen Method Man, Ghostface Killah, and Raekwon to spill dark images into your head put Wu-Tang firmly on the vision side of the line.

The genius of RZA (aka Bobby Digital) was in conceiving of a group that was *intended* to split up. Thus there was no need to contend with the perennial question of which member would split to go solo—*they all would*. True to form, in the first seven years after their debut *Enter the Wu-Tang (36 Chambers)*, the group split twice, released thirteen solo projects, and reunited for the double CD *Wu-Tang Forever*. RZA mined the audio archives to provide tracks for damn-near twenty CDs and did the score for the samurai epic *Ghostdog* on the side. The irony of Wu-Tang lay in the fact that with nine MCs, they had no room for the parade of "guest" rappers that were a virtual marketing requirement for artists from the early 90s onward. And this wasn't solely because there were simply too many of them to fit anyone else in the mix, but also because the Wu-Tang aesthetic was so eccentric, singular, and fingerprinted that those releases that did feature outside artists tended to come off as distractions.

The Evidence: Check the perfectly pitched collaboration of Raekwon and Inspectah Deck on the classic "C.R.E.A.M." from the debut *Enter the Wu-Tang (36 Chambers)* or the onomatopoetic "Careful" on the third release, *The W*. Backed by a murky, narcotic track just this side of trip hop and an intermittent lamenting horn, the cut is vintage Wu-Tang. The morosely tight production work is matched by Ghostface Killah's talent for delivering custom-fit non sequiturs. Try wrapping your brain around a Ghostface gem like "I ran the dark ages/Constantine the Great, Henry the VIII/Built with Genghis Khan and rocked suede polygons." Or the deft irrelevancies like "These are the bones of Houdini/Ronzoni noodles sprinkled on your enemy," which were delivered with a straight face. Short of the manic, acid-trip rants produced by Ol' Dirty Bastard, Ghost's lines are the most enigmatic references in a group that specializes in lyrical obscurity. The highest expression of Wu-Tang's lyrical insularity, of course, was the blistering "Triumph" on their uneven double release *Wu-Tang Forever*. The single featured all nine of the original roster in addition to utility rapper Capadonna delivering lines over a thickly bassed, string-laden track.

Part of the group's appeal—and their enigma—lay in their deliberately oblique references to 5% theology—the teachings of Clarence 13X, the Harlem mystic who broke away from the Nation of Islam and created his own movement. But a larger part had to do with their signature sound. Not only were they lyrically distinct, but RZA's production work was equally eccentric. Characterized by off-center elliptical sounds and a palette of uncommon audio effects—like the digital wail that dominates his track for "Hollow Bones"—RZA's aesthetic was the perfect companion for the content of the Staten Islanders holding down the mic.

Wu-Tang was part of a complement of New York–based artists attempting to resurrect their city's battered reputation. Among those verbal warriors, the prodigy Nasir Jones, known to the world alternately as Nasty Nas, Nas Escobar, and simply Nas, was arguably the most significant. Stark. Haunting. Illuminating in cold light. *Illmatic*, the 1994 debut release, was all of the above and more. The album could've been called *Ill Cinematic* both because of his references to flicks and the damn-near three-dimensional imagery offered by the twenty-year-old lyricist. Nas mentioned down the line that his game plan had been to make *Illmatic* and then go to film school—which might explain his cinematic approach to narration. It was no coincidence that a line from "One Love"—"Shorty's laugh was cold blooded/as he cracked a smile/only twelve tryin to tell me that he liked my style"—inspired a scene in the Hype Williams feature *Belly*.

He offered a coy double entendre in the title of his most noted track, "It Ain't Hard To Tell." And you could've seconded the notion that it literally wasn't hard to tell that this was a superior artist—as well as the implied statement about his gift for effortless narration. Except that sometimes it *was* hard to tell. The listener didn't know whether Nas was a natural-born prodigy or if he just started earlier and stayed up later.

The young verbalist was most often compared to the masterful Rakim, who had employed his early musical training as the basis of his MC style. The same might've been said for Nas. It wasn't widely played at the time that he was the son of the blues musician Olu Dara or what the impact of that relationship on his music had been. (A later installment titled "You're Da Man" confessed that rap was "our version of the blues.") Nas lays his cards on the table in the father-son collaboration "Bridging The Gap," but for the bulk of *Illmatic* he allows the reader to believe he literally came out of nowhere, a dispassionate observer of a world spinning crookedly on it axis. This was ironic because more than any subsequent piece of his work, *Illmatic* channeled the blues ethos that ran through his Mississippi-born father's music. The LP was defined by a jaded project ennui, an old-too-soon kind of lyricizing that said as much about Nas as it did the people he was describing. That might be the reason that the opening track was titled "New York State of Mind." He does not offer condemnation, judgment, or glorification, but rather the razor details of a lucid dream. At the same time, he was a twenty-year-old with bravado to spare, telling us he had come into this world by shooting his way out of the womb. Remember, this was the same artist whose public reputation was birthed by a single line delivered on Large Professor's collaboration "Live at the Barbeque":

> *Verbal assassin, my architect pleases*
> *When I was twelve, I went to hell for snuffin' Jesus*

For all the praise it inspired, *Illmatic* was a relatively short album, ten songs that occupied less than an hour of playing time. But like the economical poetry of the artist who produced it, the album wasted nothing. Taken in total, *Illmatic* was a snapshot—not a portrait—of home where airbrushing would make the image worse, not better. "One Love" speaks of a failed hood who finds himself behind bars and still not free from the drama of projects he left behind. "Memory Lane" charts the tribulations of a past that cannot be distant because the narrator himself is so young. But however recent it may have been in actual minutes, hours, and days, you also can't escape the notion that he speaks of events that are, nonetheless, centuries bygone.

But even more interesting is the snapshot of the artist as a young man. He did not deliver that single photo album and depart the field to pursue film. Instead he crafted *It Was Written* and then *I Am*, releases that saw him on a high wire, balancing the kind of sophisticated artistry that had made him famous ("The Message") with the kind of popular concerns that would make him increasingly wealthy.

For what it matters, Nas's trial was not unique—which either makes his situation understandable or that much more incomprehensible depending upon how large your heart is. Kool G. Rap's demise came specifically when he was trading in his stockpile of similes for bland gangsta catch phrases. G. brought to hip hop an unprecedented density of rhyme on bangers like "It's a Demo" and "Poison," but the post-1992 G. Rap had only "Ill Street Blues" to point to as evidence of his lyrical worth in his deluge of West Coastisms. Nas is a student of history, so his trip to the stark side on his later releases became a riddle that much more complex.

Nas would later audaciously claim the title God's Son—a sure irony for one who came into the hustle claiming to have slapped Christ himself. But this is the difference between a twenty-year-old mic prodigy and a man nearing the age of Jesus at Calvary. In hip hop, the gem-encrusted crucifix is the accessory du jour for the thug on the make—an homage that would be way beyond the humble means of a Nazarene carpenter. But these are men who relate to Jesus not as divine savior or dispenser of eternal grace, but on the level of their common understanding of what it feels like to be fucked with by those in authority.

To be precise, Jesus is real as racial profiling.

Whatever the case was to become, the Nas of *Illmatic* was not preoccupied with such spiritual vagaries. The comparisons to Rakim ended when it came to metaphysical concerns. On *Illmatic* he offered only the redeeming value of having told the truth. His specific skill at urban portraiture, at depicting a textured, if bleak concrete landscape, made the listener take note on *Illmatic*. In succeeding years, as the music became increasingly preoccupied with hyperbole and bold-faced exaggeration, Nas's youthful clarity on *Illmatic* became even more noteworthy as an example of what truthful hip hop could sound like. Whether or not truth mattered, ultimately, was a question he left to others to answer. The truth would neither set you free nor make you sick. It simply was. And for hip hop, at that delicate moment, that was redemption enough.

Hip hop had never been a model of ideal gender relations. But in the Modern Era, a kind of clitoral shtick became central to the female artists—as typified by the emergence of Trina, Foxy Brown, and Lil'

Kim. These were easily the three most (commercially) recognized female MCs if you place an asterisk next to the genius–earth mother Lauryn Hill. Where earlier women had broadened the range of the discussion during the Golden Age, in the subsequent period, the content of female rappers had been telescoped down to a cliché audioporn. On one
level, that kind of hyperbolic heterosexuality was predictable: the tired
label of *lesbian* had been consistently hurled at female artists who operated in the testosterone-suffused spaces of hip hop. The gods of commercial calculation ensured that the mics would next be passed to a roster of ghetto-fabulous nymphs so enamored with all things phallic that
their orientation could not be questioned. That tendency became so entrenched that in the early millennium, an unquestionable talent like
Jean Grae could languish in obscurity because she didn't fit into any rel-
evant commercial (read: sexual) slot.

MC Lyte has pointed out that female artists within hip hop saw
their individual popularity and influence increasingly tied to that of the
male collective they were attached to. Foxy Brown owed her initial rip-
ple to the support of Jay-Z and later Nas, AZ and Nature in the rhyme
posse the Firm. Lil' Kim made her way into the arena via the support
and microphone endorsements of Notorious B.I.G. and later the Junior
M.A.F.I.A. Even the early and mid-90s West Coast acts Yo-Yo and Lady
of Rage were creatively midwifed by Ice Cube's Lench Mob and Dr.
Dre's Death Row roster. The MCs Isis and Queen Mother Rage were
both attached to the Blackwatch Movement (and more specifically the
Nubian pimp overlords X-Clan). For better or worse, these female
artists had followed the same pattern established by the Funky Four's
addition of Sha-Rock nearly fifteen years earlier.

By contrast, Lyte's reputation as an MC overshadowed that of her
artistic (and biological) siblings, the Audio Two. Latifah was easily the
dominant artist of the Jersey-based Flavor Unit and a creative equal in
the Afrocentric-tinged Native Tongues ensemble. She could also lay
claim to the unprecedented distinction of having discovered and shep-
herded the careers of other significant acts, most notably Naughty by
Nature and Monie Love.

It's possible, though not easy, to look at the music during these
years and understand it for what it was, not what it represented. In recent hindsight, that era of music is defined by the warring East and
West Coast camps, conflict that culminated in fratricide on both sides.
The careful observer, however, would have to note that in the span of

only two albums, three discs if you're being pedantic, Notorious B.I.G. had basically redefined the art of storytelling within hip hop and that Tupac had elusively managed to become the most revered or rappers on the strength of his convictions—meaning both his beliefs and his incarcerations—if not on the mechanics of flow or elusive punchlines. However you quantify the legend he lived, his art ushered in an era in which MCs could exist beyond, beneath, and outside their own pretensions. In short, allowing them to tell the truth.

Though not spoken of in the same terms, the advent of Southern artists like OutKast, Goodie Mob and Scarface, and the Chicago-based Common Sense during that era indicated that hip hop was in fact a national (and increasingly international) music and the long-neglected regions of the country had graduated past their respective old schools and gone down new artistic paths. It could also be said that hip hop artistry was unabashedly connected to the concerns of the market; the once broad array of voices, styles, and worldviews that defined the previous era increasingly contracted into a gangsterism of clichés. The self-prophesied and violent deaths of both Shakur and B.I.G. were never supposed to have happened in the culture where battling was verbal and murders metaphorical.

Hip hop, in its third decade, unquestionably became a global phenomenon. The unparalleled influence of industry corporations on what was produced, heard, and understood as "hip hop" predictably produced a backlash—one which sought clear demarcation of "underground" versus "commercial" music. Looking at the divide within the music in this era it would be hard to believe that there was once a time when pop acts like Jazzy Jeff and the Fresh Prince could open at hardcore hip hop spots like Union Square or the Latin Quarter. On one level, the fetishization of the "underground" was like swearing allegiance to an imaginary homeland. The 50 Cent who once declared himself king of the self-produced, street-corner sold mixtape was the same 50 Cent who titled his debut *Get Rich or Die Tryin'*, which sold multiple millions of units.

That romance for a hip hop untainted by market forces was probably the reason that freestyle, the art of lyricizing from the top of one's head, experienced a resurgence during the era. The irony of that lays in the fact that freestyling was introduced to a broader audience via the 2002 Eminem biopic *8 Mile*—and that audience promptly accepted it as the hallmark of the true MC. The irony of this need not be pointed out. But then again, maybe it does. Engels famously stated that a capitalist would sell a mob the rope they use to hang him. And a century and a half later, commerce would be in a position to define what was and was not commercial. (The inside joke being that *everything* was commercial.) A win-win scenario for the barons whose marketing of "underground" acts was sort of like a dictator getting to design his own opposition party.

While the regionalization of hip hop had been underway for over a decade, it was not until that late 1990s that the South emerged as a dominant commercial factor in the music. That development could be placed almost squarely on the shoulders of OutKast. Future generations of hip hop heads will no doubt debate whether OutKast or A Tribe Called Quest were the most consistent in terms of the quality of their work, but what is beyond question is OutKast's role in crafting the Southern aesthetic.

It might have to be said that the term *Southern* is, in itself, misleading. Between 1998 and 2005, the city of Atlanta alone produced groundbreaking artists with a frequency that had not been seen since the Golden Era. In that span of time, it could lay claim to diverse and influential acts like Ludacris, Lil' Jon, Goodie Mob, T.I., Yin Yang Twins, and Killer Mike.

Atlanta also became the epicenter for the distinctive, though lyrically simple approach known as *crunk.* Defined as the Dirty South conjugation of the word *crank,* the crunk movement was spearheaded primarily by Lil' Jon and an array of mainly Atlanta-based artists like Yin Yang Twins and Bone Crusher. Crunk's appeal lay in its reliance upon methodical, bone-rattling, bottomed-out rhythms and elemental shouted chants. At a point when other regional artists were attempting to create increasingly intricate R&B hooks to fasten their lyrics to, crunkists moved in the opposite direction, slowing the music down and literally yelling catch phrases. At the same time, the Houston-based DJ Screw pioneered a laced out approach to the music, featuring elongated rhythms dragging like a West Texas drawl. It was, in a word, *Screwed.* It was said that the music mirrored the glazed world of syrup-sippers—the stimulant adventurers who took to drinking codeine cough syrup for its intoxicating effects.

Less noticed was a small but significant mid-western movement fronted by artists like Kanye West, Twista, and Common (Chicago), Nelly (St. Louis), and Eminem and Obie Trice (Detroit). That movement was not held together by a common aesthetic tendency—Common and

Nelly have scarcely more than a time zone in common. The significance lay in the fact that hip hop's regionalization was complete—so much so that 50 Cent's G-Unit could feature artists from New York, Tennessee, and California without coming off as a United Nations of the rap world. Then again, this could also indicate the extent to which the market had become the primary force in the direction of the music. A tri-regional rap act—fronted by a certified NYC thug who rapped with a Southern drawl—would be a marketing director's dream.

Of that body of Midwest-produced rap, Kanye West's *College Dropout* and Common's *Be* were arguably the most aesthetically important. By 2004, when *Dropout* was delivered, hip hop had largely devolved into a circular firing squad, riddled with gangster clichés and potboiler tales of the alleged hood. (If the words *rims, Benz, nine-millimeter, bitches,* and *benjamins* were removed from the lexicon, 90 percent of the artists from that era would be left mute.)

College Dropout forced its audience to ask, When it had last seen a rapper self-assured enough to crack a joke on a record. The comedic asides on *Dropout* were the funniest offering since Biz-Markie redefined the art of singing on 1989's "Just a Friend."

On intro track, "We Don't Care," Kanye manages to lampoon both ersatz gangsterism and saccharine odes to community uplift at the same time, announcing he has the "perfect song for the kids" before crooning, "All my people that's drug dealing just to get by, stack your money 'til it gets sky high." On "Workout" he turns in a cameo as a self-help guru, offering a regimen to help hefty women "pull a rapper, a NBA player, or at least a dude with a car." Between tracks, he offers comic op-eds on the futility of higher education, such as "No, I've never had sex, but my degree keeps me satisfied."

Bear in mind, this is the same cat heard blatantly praising the Lord on "Jesus Walks" and rapping to the spirit of his girlfriend's deceased father on the spiritual balm "Never Let Me Down." And this first jewel warrants further exploration. Issuing verses over a drumroll and intermingled gospel vocals, West turns in lines like "I don't think there's nothing I can do to right my wrongs/I wanna talk to God, but I'm afraid 'cause we ain't spoke in so long." Compare that to hip hop's traditional rendering of God as the divine baller ensuring that one's digits remain large and bitches in line and you can see the significance of that release.

And, yes, the cynics were right—Kanye West was never the best rapper going—but then again, he didn't have to be. He had enough conceptual originality and wit to get over with the middle-range flow that he has. (He had skills enough that lyrical masters Talib Kweli and Common didn't lose him on their collaboration "Get 'em High," neither.) This is stylistic synergy—the way Joe Louis wasn't particularly quick or especially powerful or evasive, but his total package of skills was lethal. He harks back to that old neglected tradition of the MC as party entertainer. He didn't set out to be the next Big Daddy Kane—or Kane's lyrical descendant Jay-Z for that matter. West was the 2.0 version of the party rapper whose lineage stretches way back to the days of Busy Bee, Biz, and Slick Rick.

Part of the appeal of this CD is the fact that it was entirely crafted by a single producer and has a musical continuity that was damn-near absent from hip hop in the era of the multi-produced, niche-marketed street opus. That the sole producer is also the main rapper puts *College Dropout* in the leagues with Dre's high-water mark, *The Chronic*. And *Chronic* is basically an anthology of MCs signed to the Death Row label; Kanye enlisted multiple guest lyricists, including Mos Def, Ludacris, and fellow Windy City native Twista, but at the end of the day, he remained the sole proprietor of his shop.

It was at this point that hip hop magazine editors could, without being ironic or sarcastic, ask if lyricism even mattered within a genre that was built upon lyrical showmanship. The truth, of course, was that lyrics did and still do matter, but the fact that the question required a thoughtful pause before replying was answer enough.

3

Word of Mouth

Rapper grips mic tight
Drums explode in throat's barrel
Lyrics leap from lips
          —Joel Dias-Porter

STEP IN THE ARENA

Hemingway defined courage as grace under pressure. In the black tradition, though, grace under pressure is the definition of *cool*—which leads us to the understanding that *coolness is a form of individual courage*. No wonder, then, that in Yoruba art, the quality of mystic coolness (*itutu*) is often represented by the color blue—suggesting that existential calmness, and therefore courage, is at the heart of the blues tradition. In the hip hop arena, the battle, the ritual exchange of freestyle barbs, requires mental poise, grace under verbal fire, and composure—literally. Here we witness the rapid-fire calculation of speed chess combined with the language virtuosity of a poetry recital.

The concept of the hip hop battle is the obvious extension of "the dozens," snapping, riffing, breaking, jonin', dissin': the ritual insults of the black vernacular tradition. The folklorist Roger D. Abrahams pointed out that

> the practice of mother-rhyming (the dozens) has been observed in various Afro-American communities as well as in a number of groups in Africa, including the Yoruba, Efik, Dogon, and some Bantu tribes.

And inside this sphere of formalized disrespect, coolness is the ultimate virtue because he who loses his temper loses face, the contest of wits, and sometimes teeth. Mel Watkins's history of black comedy *On the Real Side* points out that

> when confined to friends and familiar circumstances [the dozens] was viewed much like a basketball or baseball game, as competitive sport. If, however, one of the limitations was ignored—say, someone appeared with his girlfriend and his manhood was questioned—the game could escalate into hostility and violence.

To battle in hip hop—or in the dozens—is to put one's name on the line and test one's self in the crucible of verbal conflict. The freestyle is the crucial element of hip hop, but also is a cornerstone of black culture that is in consistent rebellion against the strictures of form and convention. Thus what the MC calls freestyle the jazz musician calls improvisation–literally confronting structure with a riff on time. The kinesthetic genius of an NBA baller lies in his ability to construct *physical* freestyles, rebelling against the step-dribble-shoot simplicity of structure with an improvised use of body and time. This emphasis upon freedom of form emerges in direct relation to a group of people whose history has been defined by physical and time constraints. *Free* style—as in the opposite of *slave* style, understood? Beyond all else, the ability to freestyle, the ability to verbally snap the larynx of a rival MC in the crucible of the battle, is what separates the grown men from the juveniles. Doubt hip hop's literary merit if you wish, but James Baldwin never had to essay head-to-head against Norman Mailer, Eldridge Cleaver, or William Styron while sitting at the desk next to him.

Lyrical improvisation has its origins in the worksongs from which the blues sprung. Classics like "Wake Up Dead Man" or "Berta, Berta" were improvised songs built around the percussion of the hammer falling on the railroad track being laid. But the hip hop freestyle is spoken—not sung—and there is less room for verbal error in speech. The AAB structure common in blues is directly connected to the improvised nature of many of these songs; repetition of the first line gives the singer a moment to come up with the rhyming punchline in the third. But the freestyle rapper gets no breathers. The MC is in constant, literal dialogue with not only the audience but also their collective sense of timing and expectation.

Ralph Ellison—whose own word craft was informed by the temporal sensibilities he developed as a musician—riffed on the uses of time in the prologue to *Invisible Man,* a statement that also speaks to the nature of the MC craft.

> Once I saw a prizefighter boxing a yokel. The fighter was swift and amazingly scientific. His body was one violent flow of rapid rhythmic action. He hit the yokel a hundred times while the yokel held up his arms in stunned surprise. But suddenly the yokel, rolling about in the gale of boxing gloves, struck one blow and knocked science, speed and footwork cold as a well-digger's posterior . . . the yokel has simply stepped inside his opponent's sense of time.

Nelson George once observed that the *battle royale* in the opening pages of *Invisible Man* bore a relationship to hip hop's element of battle. But the parallel of the pugilist to the MC also exists on a level beyond simple metaphors. It makes sense that Muhammad Ali, the boxer with the most highly cultivated and idiosyncratic understanding of time inside the ring, was also the lyrical forerunner of the MC outside it. Jay-Z pointed this out when announcing his retirement as a rapper:

> People compare rap to other genres of music, like jazz or rock 'n' roll. But it's really most like a sport. Boxing to be exact. The stamina, the one-man army, the combat aspect of it, the ring, the stage, and the fact that boxers never quit when they should.

In hip hop we find Mike Tyson immortalized in verse like the gladiators of old (you never saw Sinatra, for instance, singing about Rocky Marciano, but you did see Joe Louis valorized in Richard Wright, Cab Calloway, and Paul Robeson's collaboration "King Joe Blues"). Sonny Liston lived his life as a blues epic: born in the Arkansas backwater, the thirteenth child, his date of birth was etched into a tree that was struck by lightning and shattered, leaving him a man without known beginnings. If Liston had not been born, the blues would've had to invent him. Tyson, though, was pure hip hop metaphor: raised in Brownsville, the crumbling precinct at the center of Crooklyn's mythology, rolling into the ring accompanied by the organized cacophony of Public Enemy's "Welcome to the Terrordome" or Redman's demented funk "Time for Some Action." And it was no coincidence that Tyson found himself in the company of hip hop personas Tupac Shakur and Suge

Knight—Pac was, in fact, leaving a Tyson fight the night he was gunned down on the Vegas strip.

In his prime, Roy Jones, Jr.—a rapper in his own right—*fought* in an improvisational style that almost seemed like the ring equivalent of a freestyle verse, which is one reason you find innumerable references to him in hip hop, but virtually none for that gentleman pugilist Lenox Lewis or the ring evangelist Evander Holyfield. The rapper and the prizefighter share the common themes of improvisation and requisite composure in the face of incoming fire. Boxing is physical entrepreneurship for the dead-broke—an arena where one's fists are the equivalent of venture capital. Hip hop is verbal offense and defense raised to the level of high art. And both the pugilist and the MC share a common charge in their professions: protect yourself at all times.

Down in the diminished wards of the City where some hearts run as cold as the (651) area code, disrespect is a form of larceny and worthy of capital punishment. The axiom holds that if you look at what people pursue in excess then you're usually looking at what they were once deprived of. In the City, respect is worth more than money—because respect is what will allow you to keep dollars in your pocket and not in the possession of those who would trespass against you. In hip hop—and inside the broken histories of black men in America—respect is the ultimate medium of exchange. And that is to say, in battling, the rapper is gambling with the most valuable commodity available: one's rep and the respect that flows from it.

Proverbs 22 will tell you that a good name is rather to be chosen than great riches, but in this arena one's rep *is* one's wealth. In the days of yore, heads battled for *names*—where losing MCs were stripped of their accumulated glory by being forced to assume a new MC name. And in the MC battle, victory belongs to the slickest dealer of disrespect. Take this tendency to treat insult as a blood felony and then pair it with the wit, invention, and genius of the Negro verbal tradition and the result is either a high-stakes art competition, where victory belongs to him of the swiftest tongue, or a prelude to black homicide. Or both, simultaneously.

There is a genealogy of conflict in hip hop, a lineage that connects the new school to the old school and the old school to whatever came before that. Kool Moe Dee versus Busy Bee, MC Shan versus KRS-One, LL Cool J versus Kool Moe Dee, Canibus versus LL, Common versus

Cube—all the way down to the fratricidal conflicts of Big versus Pac and the citywide civil warfare of Nas versus Jay-Z and Ja Rule vs. 50 Cent. And, to cop a line from De La Soul, the *stakes is high*. The verbal manslaughter KRS-One committed on "South Bronx" and "The Bridge Is Over" *ended* Shan's career and put the whole Queens MC delegation on artistic probation. Coming off the canvas from his rounds with LL, Canibus joined the U.S. Army—thinking it safer to handle live ammunition than hot microphones.

Elders to the game will point to the ancestral clash of Kool Moe Dee and Busy Bee at Harlem World in 1983 as the template for what was to come. True indeed, as KRS-One has pointed out, that battle was not simply a lyrical contest, but it was a clash of competing styles, differing approaches to the art of rapping, a smoke-filled referendum on the direction hip hop was to take. Moe Dee's lyrical decapitation of Busy Bee marked the triumph of the serious, poetic lyricist over the flamboyant showman, but that stylistic conflict has played itself out down to the current era, animating MC battles ad infinitum. The stake is always the same: the individual rep; the regard of the avenues, corners, and roads where you and your peoples dwell; and the stylistic evolution of hip hop. If one is to take the art form in new direction, you must defeat and exile its roster masters first. Regicide as a job requirement.

Nas gave light to this reality, explaining the genesis of his conflict with Jay-Z on "Last Real Nigga Alive":

> *In the middle of that, Jay tried to sneak attack*
> *Assassinate my character, degrade my 'hood*
> *'cause in order for him to be the don, Nas had to go*
> *the Gam-b-i-n-o rules I understood.*

Thus the conflict of rival poets earns comparison to the rub out of a rival boss in the tradition of Gotti's bullet-riddled ascension over Paul Castellano.

In the early years, the battle could be more metaphor than reality. At the zenith of their hostilities, Kool Moe Dee and LL could be photographed together at the same industry parties. For a period in the late 80s, Big Daddy Kane and Rakim were to hip hop what Frazier and Ali had been to boxing a decade earlier, what the Yankees and Dodgers were to New York in the 1950s—two antagonists so dissimilarly gifted that they were defined by each other's talents: The slow-flowing meditative

Ra contrasting with the compact densely structured lyrical assaults of Kane. Rakim, the ascetic spiritualist from the Strong Island suburbs, Kane the flat-topped hedonist hailing from the heart of Flatbush.

But the battle devolved from figurative to literal in the early 1990s and by the time Dr. Dre attacked TV host Dee Barnes for interviewing Cube on her show *Pump It Up* the nature of lyrical conflict had changed irrevocably. Ice Cube, the ex-*Nigga with an Attitude* had traded barbs with the remaining NWA members on "No Vaseline" and "100 Miles and Running," but the 1991 Barnes assault initiated an era of physical antagonism that extended not only to one's microphone nemesis, but also to the journalists who covered the music. NWA quickly dissolved into lyrical fratricide with Dre's assault on founder Eazy-E shortly after he left the Ruthless Records label. By the time Bronx native Tim Dawg's anemic assault on NWA's "Step To Me" reached airwaves, the MC skirmishes had begun to metastasize into coastal, and ultimately lethal, conflicts.

The ascent of the squad of MCs attached to Death Row Records and the grumblings that the New York MCs had been vanquished by upstarts from the left coast gave particular significance to Notorious B.I.G.'s 1994 debut, *Ready to Die.* Those same dynamics applied to Nas's blistering debut, *Illmatic,* released that same year. The burly bard from Brooklyn anointed himself King of New York on the strength of *Ready to Die*—in the face of competition from cross-borough rivals like Nas, and the Wu-Tang standouts Raekwon and Ghostface Killah. The year 1996 witnessed both the release of Jay-Z's *Reasonable Doubt* and the murder of Tupac Shakur—a loss that changed the balance of power between the coasts. Shakur had been the most noted icon not only of West Coast hip hop, but of the music at large. Though it would take some years for the hopes to be born out, *Reasonable Doubt* heralded the arrival of another MC that showed all the potential of restoring the East Coast to its former glory. B.I.G.'s death five months after Shakur's effectively closed a chapter in which the battle had drifted far away from its roots: two turntables, one microphone; two MCs, one title, and the freestyle exchange of artistic insult. Hip hop had driven at full speed down a dead-end street and now the only route available was to move backward. The extended wake of their deaths saw the continuation of conflict among artists. But the Shakur and B.I.G. parables were at least part of the reason that subsequent conflicts—most notably Jay-Z and Nas—remained lyrically lethal, not literally so.

The ability to freestyle reached the point of diminishing returns in the era of the MC as commercial vehicle—despite, or perhaps because of, the momentary rush of attention the form received after the success of the 2002 Eminem biopic *8 Mile*. Freestyle is to hip hop as street ball is to the NBA. Just as asphalt legend has it that many a pro baller got his game dissed and dismissed on the asphalt proving grounds of Harlem's Rucker League, there is no shortage of triple-platinum-level rappers who would get *took* in the freestyle arena. This is the age-old conflict of glitz against guts, played out with the elemental tools of the hip hop trade: two turntables and a microphone. An arena where speaking a previously written rhyme—as opposed to going *extemp* from the top of the head—is treated as kindly as marking a card in a back-alley poker game. This relationship to the freestyle battle aesthetic is one of the reasons why Ice Cube, who is central to the history of hip hop, but is not and never was a *battle* rapper per se, lacked the skill to funk with Common's classic incendiary "I See the Bitch in You." Incensed by a line about West Coast on "I Used to Love H.E.R.," Common's metaphorical ode to hip hop, Ice Cube responded with an assault titled "Westside Slaughterhouse." Pulling no punches, Cube made a pun of his opponent's original stage name, charging,

> *You used to love her*
> *Now mad 'cause we fucked her*
> *Pussy-whipped bitch*
> *With no common sense.*

In hip hop terms, Cube's salvo was standard fare for verbal conflict, but nowhere near the thermonuclear reply that was "I See the Bitch in You." The point, however, was that Cube and Common existed on different planes of the MC craft—Cube primarily as a deft lyricist and songwriter and Common as an extension of the verbal gladiator tradition that stretched back to the days of old. (Conversely, at that point in their careers, Common's record as a songwriter was not nearly as impressive as Cube—who as a teen had ghostwritten virtually all of NWA's classic *Straight Outta Compton*.)

And yet the battle—as central as it is to hip hop—is only one element of what makes a great MC. Rare is the artist who was capable of operating in both of these arenas with equal adroitness. The songwriting artist with battle skills is the hip hop equivalent of ballplayer whose game is as tight on Madison Square Garden's hardwood as it is on Harlem's asphalt. Or the boxer who both hits hard and is hard to hit. It's worth noting, however, that after the turning-point release *Like Water for Chocolate,* Common was essentially reincarnated as an artist in the songwriter-lyricist mode. The Common who conceived of the conceptually bold if poorly executed *Electric Circus* in 2002 was a millennium away from the mic-ripping artist who first blew out of the Windy City a decade earlier. Taken together, lyricism and battle skills were indispensable elements of greatness, but did not constitute the total package. For the MC, the mechanics of *how* one raps have proven to be as important as the content and circumstances under which one says it.

BENEATH THE SURFACE

Those who dismissed hip hop at the outset as musically monotonous missed the point. Hip hop has its musical roots in the breakbeat or "the bridge"—the most kinetic section of a record. The first rappers floated their vocals over synchronized "bridges" provided by the DJ who had mastered the ability to repeat the most kinetic section of song ad infinitum. Instead of having a bridge within a bridge—which might have sounded less *monotonous* to the uninitiated—the variation lay within the realm of the lyricist. The primary question on the floor is what a given MC can do artistically within a 4/4 measure. And the answers to this question, as we'll see, are myriad. Though the genre will always be dismissed by many as brash, monotonous noise, the truth is that hip hop has undergone an astounding array of lyrical and musical transformations.

Early hip hop featured simple syncopation—matching beats, or more specifically *pulses* to syllables—and that explains why early rappers often paused between syllables (hip . . . hop . . . you . . . don't . . . stop) and generally rapped slower than their lyrical descendants. Given the fact that early crews were built around the DJ, not the rapper, very few individual lyricists got the chance to fully demonstrate—or cultivate—their mic skills. Instead, they worked in routines where each line of a verse might be broken down and distributed to one of four or five rappers in the crew. The rapper's place in hip hop was still evolving and they treated songs the way soul singers treated duets—basically dividing the lyrics down the middle and singing the hooks in the chorus. Given the fact that the early rhyme crews were larger than the subsequent MC cliques (the Furious Five, the Fantastic Five, the Funky Four Plus One, etc.), their approach to a song also echoed 70s soul groups like the Temptations or the Four Tops where each person contributed a different timbre to a song. It was no coincidence that these early crews often featured harmonized hooks where all four or five MCs joined in—regardless of their questionable singing abilities. The Cold Crush Brothers' early routines were not all that far removed from doo-wop. The Fantastic Five harmonized their way through entire stanzas before dissolving into rhyme:

> *We're the fantastic romantic five*
> *We're the crew that makes you come alive*
> *So when you're rockin' to the sound*
> *That the five are laying down*
> *Just dance, boogie scream and shout*
> *'cause we won't hesitate to turn it out.*

Rapping and singing were so closely related at the outset that acts like the Force MDs, who eventually came to public attention as R&B singers, actually started out as rappers. (The group was originally called the Force MCs.) "White Lines"—Grandmaster Flash and the Furious Five's anti-coke anthem—was not only important in its thematic content, but also in terms of its structure. Many of the early hip hop songs—like Kurtis Blow's "Christmas Rappin"—featured beginning-to-end, uninterrupted rhyme sessions. By contrast, "White Lines" not only featured a hook that divided the song into different sections, but also contained a structural innovation. The hook was, on alternate lines, harmonized by the five MCs or spoken by a narrator:

> *Ooooh . . . White Lines*
> *Vision dreams of passion*
> *Blowin through my mind*
> *And all the while I think of you*
> *Pipe cries*
> *A very strange reaction*
> *For us to unwind*
> *The more I see the more I do*

Something like a phenomenon
Baby
Tellin your body to come along, but white lines . . . blow away
Blow! Rock it! Blow!

Again, Flash is the first-person reference for this development:

> The Kool Herc style at the time was basically freelance talking, not nec-
> essarily syncopated to the beat. The Three of them—Cowboy, Kid Cre-
> ole and Melle Mel—came up with a style called back and forth, where
> they would be MC-ing to the beat that I would play. I'll take a sentence
> that hopefully the whole wide world knows: "Eeeny Meeny Miny Mo,
> catch a piggy by the toe." So they devised it where Cowboy might say
> "Eeeny meeny," and the Creole would say, "Miny" and then Mel
> would say, "Mo." So they would kind of bounce it around.

Big Daddy Kane made a similar point, highlighting the close connection
between R&B singing and early hip hop:

> R&B is black music; before rap, that's all we had. When you really look
> at the origin of rap, "Rapper's Delight" is [performed] over "Good
> Times," an R&B song. When cats came out, they mainly rapped over
> R&B tracks. Cold Crush, Fantastic and Master Don and the Def Com-
> mittee, these cats, when they performed were singing. The Force MDs
> [originally] were a rap group, but when they were doing their rou-
> tines, they were singing. The only time they rapped is when they
> would freestyle one by one, but the majority of their routine was
> singing. So that whole melodic thing has always played an important
> part in hip hop from the beginning.

It would take time to realize that the rapper's approach to a song was
different than that of a singer—no matter how many traits the two
shared—and that there would be no room for four-part harmony in hip
hop. By the early nineties, the harmonic tradition in hip hop had been
so long neglected that Bone Thugs-N-Harmony's vocalist approach to
the hip hop song could be seen as an innovation rather than a throwback to the styles of old.

Run DMC made use of the back-and-forth style, trading single lines
and couplets on classics like "Here We Go" and "Peter Piper"—which

is essentially a duet, rapped the way Tammi and Marvin sang "Ain't Nothin' Like the Real Thing" or "Ain't No Mountain High Enough." But by the time *Raising Hell* hit the streets in 1986, the rhyme routines were on their way out. In their absence, the vocal inflection of the rapper (or his *flow*) could come to the fore.

As group routines broke down into sequential rhyme sets, the individual rapper had more input of how he would say a particular line. Not only did he have more lines to work with, he no longer had to be concerned about whether or not his inflection would disrupt the timing of the next MC down the line. And the mechanics of what we now call *flow* quickly evolved. At its heart, flow is an individual time signature, the rapper's own idiosyncratic approach to the use of time. Flow has two basic characteristics: the division of syllables and the velocity at which they are spoken.

The rhyme is mathematic: A set of twelve syllables can be broken into combinations such as $4/4/4$, $6/4/2$, or $8/2/2$, and the skilled rapper is most often trying his best to organize his syllables in the least predictable arrangement. And this is why even the slickest of MC lyrics look sterile on the page. Rakim once predicted that an imitator was liable to break his jaw trying to recite one of the master's lines in his absence. Flow is the Rosetta stone of lyrical understanding. Since there is seldom the same number of syllables or words from one line to the next, the rapper doesn't *speak* at the same speed from one line to the next. This is lyrical long division. Rapping through a standard sixteen-bar combination, the MC has to manage an equal number of changes in pitch, inflection, and delivery—all while maintaining breath control. The craft comes down to this: the trickiness of enunciation, the constant variation of speed, the tongue-twisting elongation or contraction of words. The MC is the mathematician.

The term *flow*—and all its metaphysical implications—didn't come along by accident. The aim is to be fluid, liquid, protean in one's approach to sound. Water and blood flow, liquids take the shape of their vessels—in this case, the vessel is the particular beat composition that the MC is rhyming to. In the lexicon of the avenue, to do a solid is to show a sign of strength or commitment, but on the mic, it is not a matter of strength, but finesse.

Flow is as elemental to hip hop as the concept of *swing* is to jazz. And like the jazz musician who deliberately plays an eighth note behind or ahead of the measure, flow is the science of funking with one's expectations of time. In some instances, the pure aesthetic sheen of an MC's flow is enough to get him past all but the most severe critics. Snoop Dogg's has based his entire career on the uniqueness of his flow, not the density of rhyme or impact of his punchlines. Jay-Z's tailor-made flow is so casual and conversational that he sounds more like he's talking than rapping. Ghostface Killah's "crying style" of MCing involves tapering the end of his phrases like an overwrought man on the verge of tears, while Method Man, his crewmate in the nine-MC Wu-Tang Clan outfit has a trademark flow involving the exaggerated extension of key vowels. The hyper-active, dense lines of OutKast's Andre 3000 and Big Boi are wrought with double entendres and clever wordplay, all done at a speed just past the casual comprehension of the listener.

Now compare that emotionalism with the deliberate monotonists Guru and Rakim who approach the rhyme like actors who deliberately deadpan. The hallmark of the B-list actor is the limited palette of facial expressions, the failure to make use of his or her own physicality. But for the talented actor—a William Hurt or a Meryl Streep—that same emotional reserve is a refined technique. The gifted rapper sounds distinct in terms of timbre, use of unusual vocabulary—or common vocabulary in unusual ways—tonal variation, and timing.

Like its ancestral inspiration, the blues, the hip hop lyric is built around a series of second lines, or what is known in the craft as the punchline. So an entire hip hop song can be structured in terms of (first) premise statements followed by secondary punchlines. And no, it's not a coincidence that MCs borrowed a term traditionally associated with comedy because both the craft of rhyming and joke-telling require a flawless sense of timing—not to mention the fact that the punchline in both blues and hip hop is frequently a clever phrase designed to elicit laughter from the listener.

The lyrical punchline, like it's comedic counterpart, is where all the elements of the previous lines come together. It is the line that confounds the expectations that are established in the premise line. A traditional blues lyric may state

I'm a big fat mama with meat shaking on my bones

And then repeat:

> *Lord, I'm a big fat mama with meat shaking on my bones*

But that is a sterile statement of the obvious until the singer breaks it down that

> *Ev'ry time I shake this meat, some skinny girl lose her home*
> *(Ida Cox, "Four Day Creep," 1939)*

In this case, the punchline is technically the third line sung in an AAB song structure, but it is the second line in terms of content. Now, a classic Big Daddy Kane premise and punchline hold that

> *I won't say I'm the baddest or portray that role*
> *But I'm in the top two and my father's gettin' old.*

Generally speaking, the MC uses flow to disguise the precise location where the punchline will drop (or what it is) in the same way that comedians hide the conclusion of their jokes. But any number of rappers violate these ideals, kicking rhymes with an *anti-flow*. Some use deliberately predictable cadence as means of illustrating the punchline— if the listener knows exactly where the line's punctuation will be, the rapper then has to up the ante in terms of its creativity and impact. MCs like Rass Kass, Canibus, Eminem, Lord Finesse, and his late Harlemite collaborator Big L were masters of this approach. The listener is clear almost from the outset about *where* the punchline will be, but the real question is *what* exactly it will be in terms of content. This verbal tactic is the reason that early DJs started the tradition of dropping the audio at the end of every fourth or eighth measure—to literally give the MC breathing room, to allow him to drop his punchline a capella for maximum impact. On his classic "La Di Da Di," Slick Rick—a comedic performer by nature—had his partner Doug E. Fresh drop the fourth bar to deliver his sharpest lines in a song about a mother and daughter literally fighting over his amorous attentions:

> *I tried to break it up*
> *I said "Stop it, leave her."*
> *She said "If I can't have you*
> *She can't either."*

The final phrase uttered by the jealous mother is said without musical accompaniment.

In the original proving grounds of the art form, the freestyle battle and the live-on-the-street performance, the punchline was indispensable to getting a crowd open. And under those raucous circumstances, the nuances of flow might be easily lost on the audience. Both Finesse and Big L—along with punchline kings like Rass Kass, Talib Kweli, Common, Wordsworth, and Chino XL—were direct descendants of that lineage of early playground MCs. The difference between them and their mic-gripping forbears though is that there were different criteria in the modern era, where a rapper could gain a national audience without ever matriculating through the boulevard ranks. At the same time, the rise of hip hop as commercial music made the distinction between the MC as rhyme-spitter and the MC as songwriter that much more clear. Thus began an entire lineage of MCs like Lord Finesse, Rass Kass, Supernatural, Canibus, Big L, and the legendary Mikey D, who mentored the adolescent LL Cool J in the ways of the rhyme, whose microphone skills were beyond question but who was not able to compose *songs* that were nearly as compelling as their individual rhymes. In short, the intricacies of content and flow that were so essential to success in the venues where hip hop was born were necessary but by no means sufficient in the new era.

Flow is not about *what* is being said so much as *how* one is saying it. And while any list of the greatest MCs would include at least two of the preceding names, a list of the greatest songwriters in the tradition probably would not. A Tribe Called Quest's "Electric Relaxation," for instance, contained almost no notable punchlines, but is still regarded as a classic within the genre. And it is ironic that none of the catalog of artists listed above is known for compelling lyrical flow (and, in the case of Talib Kweli, his tongue-twisting, stutter-step flow has been cited as a reason why his brilliant work has not gotten its due acclaim).

This is not an either/or scenario: commercially recognized artists like a Jay-Z and less-hailed but nonetheless blistering wordsmiths like Black Thought and Guru have the capacity to issue slick punchlines with distinctive, magnetic flows. When Jay-Z confessed on his *Black Album* that he'd "dumbed down for his audience and doubled his dollars" he was essentially talking about de-emphasizing his punchlines— since punchlines are often evasive similes and double entendres, by diminishing them the listener didn't have to think as much. Obviously not every commercially successful song in the genre has been the result of lyrical simplification, but it takes a particular kind of talent to walk that line. (He went on to issue the revealing compliment that "If skills sold/truth be told/I'd probably be/lyrically Talib Kweli.")

The most successful artists in the field have been able to wed the witty punchline to other artistic techniques—flow in particular. As flow evolved and developed in the 1983–1992 era, so also did the structural elements of the art of MCing. Rhyme styles evolved most dramatically in the 1980s, where MCs went from the basic AAAA or ABAB rhyme schemes that had been standard to dense, multi-layered compound rhymes that augmented a rapper's flow. The *art* of MCing also began to increasingly incorporate the standard techniques of literature and poetry: alliteration, metaphor, assonance, onomatopoeia, personification, and hip hop's most prominent literary characteristics, simile, double entendre, and comparison. Run DMC's 1983 classic "Sucker MCs" inaugurated a new era in hip hop's history, but started with this couplet:

> *Two years ago, a friend of mine*
> *Asked me to say some MC rhymes.*

By the end of the decade, though, listeners had come to expect a level of lyrical complexity that made the opening lines to "Sucker MCs" sound almost Seussian. In the early 1990s, Big Daddy Kane's practiced nonchalance reigned supreme as he issued lines on "Set It Off" like:

> *Attack, react exact the mack'll move you with*
> *A strong song as long as you groove to this.*

The fact that Kane was using the same AA rhyme scheme as Run DMC was obscured by the fact that he brought an unprecedented level of internal rhyme to the field—and ran through his lines far more quickly than his predecessors. Every single word in his couplet—with the exception of the articles and a single preposition—rhymes with another word. Not only did it become more difficult generally to tell *when* a particular punchline would be dropped, it became a guessing game as to which set of words it would rhyme with. The listener is no longer waiting to hear the rhyme phrase at the end of the second line, but also the rhymes at the beginning and middle of it.

The self-professed lyrical legend LL Cool J announced his musical presence with 1984's "I Need a Beat" and simultaneously introduced a broader vocabulary palette into rap music. Sounding like he'd raided every entry in an SAT prep book, LL's reliance on polysyllabic words and uncommon allusions on the original version of 1985's "Rock the Bells"—along with T La Rock's "It's Yours"—pioneered a rhyme approach that avenue denizens termed "computer style." And the wider array of words created a wider set of lyrical possibilities. Cool J's verbal repertoire shone on riffs like:

> *During this episode vocally I explode*
> *My title is the king of the FM mode*
> *See, my volume expands to consume*
> *And my structures emote a lyrical heirloom.*

Before this point, it would have been highly unlikely that a rapper would use the words connoisseur, tympanic, impresario, pestilence, plateau, subpoena, conjecture, cranium, plagiarism, metabolism, auditory, eradicate, adversary, membrane, jugular, manuscript, and virtuoso in a single song, as LL did so boldly on the remix version "Rock the Bells."

In the mid-1980s acts like the Ultra Magnetic MCs and Eric B. & Rakim were responsible for dilating the thematic possibilities of the hip hop record. Rhyme—with the notable exception of pioneers like Afrika Bambaataa's Soul Sonic Force—had been literal and concrete; in the hands of Kool Keith of the Ultras or Rakim, subject matter became abstract, metaphysical, bordering upon the science fictional. The sonic collage that underpinned the Ultras' sublime "Ego Trippin'" was augmented by Kool Keith and Ced Gee's vague non sequiturs and random allusions. The casual gravel of Rakim's unmistakable baritone stylings on "Eric B. Is President" or "Check Out My Melody" compelled the listener to dig the slick metaphysic the MC was laying down.

But Run DMC's string of commercial successes with singles like "Sucker MCs," "King of Rock," "My Adidas," and "Rock Box" introduced into hip hop the age-old conflict of art versus commerce. The rhyme schemes NWA employed on *Straight Outta Compton* were not nearly as advanced as a representative Kane or Rakim line, but the West Coast gangstas dwarfed them in sales. Too Short's "Freaky Tales" highlighted the bass-and-synth oriented sound that would come to characterize West Coast hip hop, but his rhyme scheme was elementary. The conflict between the aesthetic and the economic is the most recurrent theme in KRS-One's body of work over the past seventeen years. KRS-One's obsession with marketing-free MCing made sense given the reality that the two highest selling artists of the decade were Vanilla Ice and MC Hammer, neither of whom warranted a second look—or, truthfully, a first one—for their rhyming abilities.

Jay-Z's highlighted this theme on *The Black Album*, rapping,

> *Truth told, I wanna rhyme like Common Sense*
> *But I did 5 mill—I ain't rhymed like Common since.*

The point being that the multi-layered meanings, wordplay, and wit that made Common's name as an MC pushed the artistic boundaries of hip hop forward, but the market demands—and rewards—simplicity. Both Jay-Z and Eminem—like Tupac and Biggie before them—managed to straddle the line between that which was sellable and that which was artistically credible, but even Jay had to concede alliteratively that he "dumbed down his lyrics and doubled his dollars."

Classic Kane showcased his trademark high-velocity enunciation on his 1989 "Wrath of Kane" (a work that was impressive on wax, not so much in person. On stage, Kane needed an oxygen tank by the time he got to the second verse). His approach to the rhyme was the artistic equivalent of running wind sprints in a labyrinth.

> *Go with the flow, my rhymes grow like an afro*
> *The entertainer Kane'll gain and never have no*
> *Problem, I could sneeze, sniffle or cough*
> *e-e-even if I stutter I'ma still come off.*

But more importantly, Kane had picked up the habit of breaking lines in the middle of a sentence, a technique called *enjambment* among the literary crowd. The idea that "Kane will never have no problem" may be a single thought, but it occupies two different lines. Kane used enjambment frequently as a verbal tactic:

> *Line by line, chapter after chapter*
> *Like a pimp on the street I gotta rap to*

> *Those who chose to oppose, friend or foes*
> *I all dispose and blow 'em out like afros.*

Kane was the cleanup rhymer on Marley Marl's famous "Symphony" and had the misfortune of following Kool G. Rap, who was probably the only rapper at the time who could match Kane on the level of rhyme density, verbal speed, and clever allusion. It may be debated eternally among hip hop aficionados as to who should have had the distinction of rhyming last over Marley's indelible keyboard-driven track. For the MC analyst, Kane and G. Rap's mic duel was a closer contest than the fabled bout between Marvelous Marvin Hagler and Sugar Ray Leonard in 1987.

The MC craft also came to utilize alliteration as a means of organizing rhymes. In 1988, Kool Moe Dee spat an alliteratively classic battle rhyme at the zenith of his hostilities with LL, riffing on his rival's initials as

> *Lower level, lack luster, last least, lip lover,*
> *lousy lame, late lethargic, lazy lemon, little logic*
> *lucky leech, liver lipped, laborious louse from a loser's lips*
> *living limbo, lyrical lapse, low life with the loud raps, boy.*

Pharoahe Monch decided to forego the standard definition of rhyming on "Hell" from his under-heralded solo debut, *Internal Affairs*:

> *Follow for now, for no formidable fights have been formed as yet*
> *Pharoah fucks familiar foes first, before following female MCs fiercely*
> *Focus upon the face that facts can be fabricated to form lies*
> *My phonetics alone forced feeble MCs into defense on the fly—feel me?*

Rakim's "Follow the Leader" was an alliterative masterpiece. Here Rakim laced his cosmic allusions with staccato consonant combinations.

> *Music mixed mellow maintains to make*
> *Melodies for MCs motivates the breaks.*

In addition to alliteration, MCs had utilized personification at least as far back as 1982 when Melle Mel offered a deft example of the technique on "New York, New York."

> *A castle in the sky, one mile high*
> *Built to shelter the rich and greedy*
> *Rows of eyes, disguised as windows*
> *Lookin DOWN on the poor and the needy.*

Mel speaks as if the building itself is looking down on impoverished people in the streets—mimicking the attitudes of the overlords who constructed them.

But given the thematic orientation of later hip hop, the personification would take on a deliberate boulevardian edge. Thus Nas on his 1996 sophomore release *It Was Written* breathes life into a Desert Eagle, semi-automatic nine-millimeter:

> *Always I'm in some shit, my abdomen is the clip*
> *The barrel's my dick—uncircumcised*
> *They pull me back and cock me*
> *I bust off when they unlock me.*

Tupac's "Me and My Girlfriend" from *Don Killimunati* extends the same theme, making his gat into his significant other.

> *Nigga, my girlfriend may be 45, but she still live*
> *One shot making Niggas heartbeat stop*
> *My girlfriend blacker than the darkest night*
> *When Niggas act bitch-made she got the heart to fight.*

Lloyd Banks's contribution to G-Unit's "8 More Miles" is a coke's-eye narration of the drug hustle:

> *You could sniff me, cut me, I'll turn you into a junkie*
> *I'm the number one seller in the whole fucking country*
> *Wall street niggas, they cop me on the low*
> *White boys, they don't call me coke, they call me blow.*

On *Return of the Boom Bap* (1993) KRS-One satirized the hip hop obsession with get-high with "I'm a Blunt," a song personifying a marijuana-filled blunt trying to avoid being smoked by a succession of rappers—ultimately being passed around to then-presidential candidate Bill Clinton.

As the form evolved, the artistic watermark for the exceptional MC rose higher and higher. MCs began experimenting with both simple and extended metaphors. De La Soul's classic 1989 *Three Feet High and Rising* featured the single "Potholes in My Lawn," an abstract metaphor tying suburban yard woes to the wholesale imitation of their artistic style. Large Professor, the South Queens producer and MC whose "Live at the Barbeque" brought an adolescent Nas to national attention, was also responsible for "A Friendly Game of Baseball" (1991), in which the routine brutality of New York City police is likened to a spectator sport. In his telling, RBI's are "real bad injuries," not runs batted in, and the game is measured in *endings*, not innings.

> *When the outfielder guns you down,*
> *You're out and off to the dugout underground.*

Brooklynite wordsmith Masta Ace paid tribute to that same theme in 2003 with "Unfriendly Game," in which the illicit drug hustle is detailed in the form of a football game. In four double-entendre laden bars, Ace lays out the playbook:

> *Your offense gotta be cats with no conscience*
> *No nonsense Niggas, with no options*
> *Who know how to carry that rock*
> *Make the hand off and run off the block.*

The meaning in his line is that the drug hustler relies upon workers not burdened by a moral conscience, but in the athletic world, the player who is able to score at will and without hesitation is lauded as having "no conscience." The reference to having "no options" means that the drug seller has no viable alternatives, but it also refers to the play-option pass in football. The latter two lines make use of the alternate meanings of the term "rock," which is avenue terminology for both crack and a ball used in sports, "hand off," which is both a play in football and the means by which low-level hustlers make hand-to-hand drug sales, and "run off the block," which could be either following one's blockers to gain rushing yardage or literally running off the block when the police arrive.

GZA, the under-heralded lyricist of the Wu-Tang Clan, breathed new life into the cliché of the city existing as a "concrete jungle" with "Animal Planet" from *Legend of the Liquid Swords*—a song on which he imagined the cast of characters in his neighborhood as animals and pondered how those animal traits played themselves out in the urban eco-system.

> *Shouldn't gamble with a cheetah and not expect to get beat*
> *You silly goose, you know he move fast on his feet*
> *Now you're neck deep in depth with a bunch of lone sharks*
> *So you move on a colony of ants with aardvarks.*

Duke Ellington famously declared that "music is my mistress" and that same sentiment animated what is probably the most respected extended metaphor in the history of hip hop, Common's "I Used to Love H.E.R.," in which he relays his relationship to hip hop as an on-again, off-again romance.

> *I met this girl when I was ten years old*
> *And what I loved most, she had so much soul*
> *She was old school when I was just a shorty*
> *Never knew throughout my life she would be there for me.*

Speaking in terms reserved for a lost love, Common narrates the rise of hip hop as the tale of a local girl whose entertainment career leads her to forget where she comes from ("Now I see her in commercials, she's universal"). What made Common's metaphor so widely hailed was the skill he utilized in conveying what had, by that point, become a very widely held view of the art form. And, on the real, the metaphor was so slickly composed that the entire second layer of meaning might have gone unnoticed to the casual listener had he not included the final line, "Who I'm talking about, y'all, is hip hop." The significance of the developing use of metaphor and extended metaphor in hip hop is hard to overstate. As with any artistic evolution, the aesthetic stakes in the form grew higher with time. The presence and utilization of time-honored literary techniques—the same stuff being pored over in Intro to English Lit classes made it increasingly difficult to defend the argument that hip hop did not qualify as art. Unapologetic and audacious as it was, hip hop had been clear about this debate from the gate. But the developing body of work had begun to make that clear to the blinkered crowds that had initially cut their eyes at this newly birthed approach to music.

By the mid-1980s, artists had begun drafting less common literary techniques and welding them into their approach to self-expression.

Epistolary form, for example, involves a narrative that is told in the form of letters being exchanged. LL Cool J's *Radio* (1985) featured the moralistic "Dear Yvette," an open letter charting the abundant trysts of a fast local girl. On *Illmatic* Nas delivered the epistolary gem "One Love"—a one-sided correspondence between the poet and a recently incarcerated friend. He Monday-morning-quarterbacks the missteps that resulted in the jail bid and gives him the headlines of events in their common 'hood before speaking of his aspirations for him when they're reunited on the outside. Tupac's *Me Against the World* contained "Dear Mama," a missive to his mother detailing the depth of his love for her, despite the trials that lay in their history together. He ends telling her

There's no way I could pay you back
But my plan is to show you that I understand.

Masta Ace's 2003 *Disposable Arts* featured the comic "Dear Diary," in which his diary, a record of his fears and self-doubts, writes *him* a letter advising him to "write your rhymes in the shower—you're washed up." In 2000 Eminem produced the haunting "Stan," a two-way exchange in which a fan gradually reveals his deteriorating mental state and the rapper responds to him—really to his fans at-large and his critics as well—telling him to distinguish between entertainment and reality.

Alliteration, personification, and metaphor came to be common in the genre, but comparison, double entendre, and simile became the central literary techniques of the hip hop lyricists—and for clear reasons. If the freestyle battle was the engine driving the evolution of MC styles, there was no easier way to establish a contrast between two vocalists than the use of comparison. At its core, the battle really was little more than a form of artistic comparison. The whole purpose of an analogy is to simplify a complex relationship—*this* (the complex thing) is like *that* (the simpler one).

In hip hop, the use of simile and analogy was from the outset used to illustrate the preternatural talents of the vocalist or the indisputable wackness of his rhyme competitor. Thus, Cypress Hill lead rapper B-Real's assertion that "you trying to step up to me for some action/ that's like Mike stepping to Papa Joe Jackson" is part of a long tradition of telling one's peers that verbal resistance is futile. *This* (a wack MC approaching me) is like *that* (a small-boned androgynous performer challenging his abusive blue-collar dad). Vintage LL similied himself to a heavyweight champ saying "I'm like Tyson, icin' I'm a soldier at war/making sure you don't try to battle me no more." Talib Kweli fore-warned any prospective foes that "I'm like shot clocks, blood clots and interstate cops—my point is, your flow gets stopped"—cleverly con-flating several different implications of the word "flow."

Busta Rhymes, verbalizing on the remix for Pharoahe Monch's in-cendiary "Get the Fuck Up," dismissed a rival by saying:

> *The bitch in you coming out and you're showing it*
> *Like when the British civil service gave secrets to the Soviets.*

Mos Def offered a classic line on the cut "Definition," from the Black Star project, claiming that the duo had "accurate assassinship" before pointing out that "me and Kweli close like Bethlehem and Nazareth." In a different vein, Nas on *Illmatic* advertised his prodigious weed con-sumption by stating

> *You couldn't catch me in the streets without a ton of reefer*
> *That's like Malcolm X catching the jungle fever.*

The ultimate homage to an MC's skill is the rewind. Only the most basic of MCs can be taken at face value; the true artist strives to craft rhymes that, like a taut cinematic thriller, you understand better the sec-ond time around. And this effect can be achieved in a number of ways—an intricate flow, filled with unexpected rhyme phrases may induce re-peat listening. But more often than not, MCs prefer to drop lines with layered meanings that filter up to the surface five seconds after the line was spoken—when the listener is already grappling with the next rhyme phrase. This explains why simile is so frequently paired with an-other of the MC's trademark lyrical tools—the double entendre.

On "Dooinit" from the *Resurrection* LP, Common offers this example:

> *I stay focused like Gordon Parks when it's sorta dark*
> *For niggas flooded with ice, my thought is the ark.*

His simile is combined with an internal rhyme and *two* double enten-dres—focus as mental concentration and as the means a photographer uses to achieve clarity in an image. Ice serves as a reference to both frozen water and diamonds. But by the time these multiple interpreta-tions become apparent, Common is already off to other subjects. And thus, a listener rewinds. Nas on *Illmatic* issued the politically incorrect simile–double entendre saying "my style switches like a faggot." Lord Finesse informed the world that "my style is tricky—like spelling Mississippi." On the classic "Raw," Big Daddy Kane constructed a simile connected to a homonym saying of his competitors that

> *None of them can see me*
> *I leave 'em whinin' like their names were BeBe and CeCe.*

The fact that the ebonic enunciation of *whining* is almost indistinct from the gospel singers' last name, *Winans*, allowed Kane to get away with an otherwise unworkable line.

While the goal of the simile is to literally express similarities between two objects or ideas, hip hop lyricism also makes use of comparisons that serve the exact opposite purpose—to highlight the *distinctions*, often between an artist and his or her inferior counterpart. In the palette of hip hop literary techniques, comparison is, in fact, behind only metaphor and simile as the method of choice. Given the simple fact that hip hop has been both explicitly and implicitly about competition since the days when the first MC dropped the first rhyme, it makes sense that comparison—especially of one's rhyming repertoire—would occupy a central niche. Phife's declaration that he "got more rhymes than the Winans got family," is grand comparison to those who know the size of that gospel-singing clan. And that point might be outdone only be KRS-One's assertion that he "got more rhymes than there's Jamaicans in Brooklyn"—you don't need a census tract to know that there's a whole lot of Jamaicans in Brooklyn.

When Jay-Z informed his listeners that "the boy got more sixes than first grade," he was talking about 600 series Mercedes Benzes, not school-aged children. G-Unit's Lloyd Banks dropped a similarly numerical theme, claiming that he "Got more four five's and nines than a deck of cards," playing on the caliber of his .45 and 9 millimeter handguns. Young Z schooled would-be contenders that he rolls with "more niggas than the NAACP"—at last count, the National Association for the Advancement of Colored People had half a million members. In that same vein, Lord Finesse announced in a classic freestyle:

> *It's better that you chill and max with me*
> *I'm sending out warnings quicker than a fax machine.*

While Big L, Finesse's partner in the revered Diggin in the Crates crew, rhymed that:

> *I keep the women screaming and fiendin' for cool shit*
> *My rhymes are phat and yours are thin as a pool stick.*

Jean Grae played on the dual meanings of the term "credit" in saying that because her skills have gone unrecognized there's "more credit due to me than a store that doesn't exchange." Grae was also responsible for a line in which she declared herself "more necessary than violence on the Amistad." M-1 of Dead Prez explained that "I be what John Wilkes Booth was to Lincoln." Wordsworth combined a slick double entendre with his comparison, pointing out that conflicts with him "result in more cast appearances than a thousand actors." In that same vein, Big Pun rhymed:

> *My prerogative to chase girls who look provocative*
> *Terror Squad rock ice whiter than Yugoslavians.*

In so doing he deliberately compared the clarity of his diamonds with the fair skin of Eastern Europeans.

Hip hop utilizes literary technique even down to its most fundamental level: the use of rhyming phrases. That rhyme is a literary technique in itself so obvious that it is overlooked. But the MC goes beyond operating on the most basic approach to rhyme—linking a single syllable to one that sounds similar to it—and employs the variations of rhyme types: oblique rhyme, double and triple rhyme, assonance, identical rhyme, and internal rhyme. Check Obie Trice's debut album, *Cheers*. On the intro track, "Average Man," the Detroit-based bard drops a swift double rhyme and follows it with a triple rhyme.

> *I'm no gangster—I'm an average man*
> *But damn if I let 'em do me savage man*
> *Before that, I'm strapped and will challenge him*
> *Cock back and the gat will damage them.*

Double rhyme entails matching two syllables to two similar sounding syllables and triple rhyme involves the same approach to three syllables. The words "average" and "savage" in the first couple constitute a double rhyme, but in order to make it work, the MC has to elide the first word down to two syllables: "av'rage." The words "challenge" and "damage" are oblique rhymes—meaning words that do not rhyme, but are enunciated in such a way as to manufacture a rhyme, but they are each attached to the proper rhymes *him* and *them.* Jay-Z worked that same technique on "Moment of Clarity."

> *Pop died, didn't cry didn't know him that well*
> *Between him doing heroin and me doing crack sales.*

The words *well* and *sale* rhyme obliquely, purely because the artist chose to blend the short *e* in "well" into *a* long a sound so the word was pronounced more like "wail."

When Jay-Z announced that "Truth be told, I wanna rhyme like Common Sense/(But I did five mil) I ain't rhymed like Common since," he was not only speaking of the corrupting influence of the dollarism on art and making deft use of homonyms, but also utilizing a technique called *identical rhyme*—the use of two words that are pronounced the same but spelled differently and carry different meanings. Kanye West uses the same identical rhyme approach on "Never Let You Down" from *College Dropout,* but follows it with a double entendre:

> *I can't complain what an accident did to my left eye*
> *'cause look what an accident did to Left Eye*
> *First Aaliyah, now Romeo must die.*

The phrases "left eye" and "Left Eye" refer to his face—which was damaged in a car accident—in the first instance and the lyricist Lisa Lopez—who was killed in a car accident—in the second. He then refers to the death of R&B singer Aaliyah and the film she starred in, *Romeo Must Die.* But it wasn't a coincidence that the television actor Romeo Santana had also been murdered in the previous year. Obie Trice on *Cheers* also utilizes identical rhyme:

> *They say to increase the peace*
> *The only piece that increase*
> *Is the type that deletes your peeps.*

The MC deliberately conflates peace, the absence of conflict, with piece, the street reference for a weapon. As in the kind of "piece" that deletes the presence of one's people.

Yet even as rhyming complexity evolved as a hallmark of hip hop lyricism, it was—at least to many on the music's periphery—overshadowed by the broad palette of words that artists chose to employ in their lyricism. To be precise: rap's insistent, widespread, and unrepentant usage of cuss words distinguished it from virtually every other popular music since the advent of rock and roll. It also gave fuel to those who would offhandedly dismiss the art form. In its early expressions, especially those captured on wax, the curse word was the rare exception. As late as the mid 1980s, Craig-G—who later earned a rep as a freestyler supreme—lamented on "Shout":

> *On the mic I don't curse, that is the worst*
> *I don't wanna catch beef every time I converse.*

Schoolly D's "PSK"—short for Park Side Killers—contained the word "fuck" and the critic and pioneer hip hop scribe Nelson George talked about how chilling the song was in its description of casual violence. The lyrical god Rakim never cursed on his classic material, and only used the word *nigga* on the cut "Know the Ledge" on the soundtrack of the film *Juice*—and even then he was rhyming in the person of the film's antagonist, Bishop (which also happened to be Tupac Shakur's breakout role). It might've been the recognition of the change in the expectations of the MC that inspired Ra to say on the Jay-Z/Dr. Dre/Rakim collaboration, "The Watcher":

> *You could try copin'*
> *I seen enough shit to leave your frame of mind broken.*

As late as 1988 Kane had to issue a disclaimer before cussin:

> *If you were loungin' around it's time to get up*
> *Pardon my expression, but I'ma tear shit up.*

(Admittedly he did say later on that same cut that you could "fuck around with Kane and come out black and blue.") The standards for lyrical audacity changed in the latter part of the 1980s, amplified in part by NWA's early releases and Ice Cube's multiple *motherfuckers* per minute ratio on *Amerikkka's Most Wanted*. Classic Cube inaugurated a song with the observation:

> *Goddamn another fucking payback with a twist*
> *The motherfuckers shot, but the punks missed.*

Ultimately, the shift meant little in terms of the mechanics of rhyming—*fuck* rhymes with *truck* no better or worse than *stuck* does—but the new language ensured that the music would not be inter-generational. Any honest reading of the musical history of black America would yield that the sentiments expressed in hip hop were not new—they were simply the first generation that could speak them without the euphemism of metaphors. On another level, the four-letter vocabulary that increasingly entered the rap lexicon served to place their poetry on the level of the context that it was more often than not attempting to describe. For what it matters, Paul Lawrence Dunbar, who caught grief from certain quarters of the afrostocracy for his use of Negro dialect in his poems, could've understood the criticisms leveled at rappers for their language liberties. As it stood, hip hop became the only music in which one might routinely hear technical nouns like *motherfucker*. But like it or not, the addition of profanity-laced lyrics echoed the ways in which some ideas were expressed. This was either evidence of either degeneracy or democracy. Or both. And on that level, maybe *fuck* did rhyme better than any of its milder substitutes.

And beyond utilizing specific literary techniques within a song, hip hop increasingly developed lyricism in which the song *was* the technique. That is to say songs that contain themes that in turn dictate how the song can be expressed. A prime example of this thematic approach is Mos Def's "Mathematics," in which the entire song is a form of algebraic expression with lines like:

> *I got 16 to 32 bars to rock it*
> *But only 10% of profits*
> *Ever see my pockets.*

"Two Words," the collaboration of Kanye West, Mos Def, and Freeway, featured three MCs organizing their verses in such a way that each two words expressed a complete thought or a complete premise for the next two words of the rhyme. Jay-Z's "22 Twos" from *Reasonable Doubt* was structured such that the words *to*, *two*, and *too* appeared twenty-two times in the first sixteen bars and 50 Cent's "21 Questions" posed that number of interrogative statements in the body of the song. Notorious B.I.G. constructed the hustler's how-to guide "Ten Crack Commandments" in such a way that the song could be divided into ten distinct themes.

Not all of these songs were based on numerical progressions. Nas scripted "Rewind," which, in keeping with the title, relayed a violent chain of events in reverse order, complete with inverted quotes like "Go he there." Masta Ace strung alphabetic lines together on "Alphabet Soup"—a song where single letters are deployed creatively to narrate the tale of a car jacking gone awry.

On virtually every level of the form—from the timing and cadence of rhymes to the level of technical sophistication in their construction—hip hop remained in dialogue with ancestral poetic and musical traditions. And at the same time, the MC remains at the foreground of those traditions, expanding their application to a new set of musical practices. In reality, though, the lyrical construction of the art was only one level on which the evolution of the art and this ancestral dialogue occurred. The other level involved the actual *content* of the work itself.

4

Asphalt Chronicles

Hip Hop and the Storytelling Tradition

Those of us who learned to write from the blues are to be envied, and those of us who have since forgotten the lessons are to be pitied.

—Murray Kempton, "Bessie Smith: Poet"

To hear it told in certain corners of his native hood, the Notorious B.I.G.'s crime epic "Niggas Bleed" was either a work of deft urban fiction or some sublime boulevard journalism with the names changed to protect those who plead innocent. In either case, it is not the kind of story that comes with that stamp of authenticity: Based on True Events. The MC, almost by musical necessity, comes down firmly on the art-imitating-life side of the equation. Had traditional fiction been his bag, there would be no question as to where the creator of the above tale was coming from, no doubt as to the genre angle he was working. But his was a different route. "Niggas Bleed"—the eleventh track on his presciently classic sophomore album, *Life After Death*—might be the signal achievement of an artist who helped redefine hip hop's storytelling tradition.

A masterpiece of lyrical economy, the song relays the detailed exploits of a hustler trying to come up on his grand score. In a single verse, he conveys an entire introduction:

Today's agenda: Got the briefcase up in the Sentra
Go to room 112. Tell 'em Blanco sent ya.

The protagonist has been charged with delivering a suitcase to a hotel room for a kingpin named Blanco. Moments later we hear the boss caution him that the recipients of that bag are known killers: "these cats you fucking with will put bombs in your mom's gas tank." Undeterred, the character schemes on a robbery that will make him rich and enlists a maniacal killer named Arizona Ron as an accomplice. Outnumbered and outgunned, the pair set a fire reckoning that "when they evacuate, they meet their fate." The resulting scene is not G-rated.

As soon as they hit the door
We start blastin
Brains hit the floor
Ron's laughin.

The Notorious B.I.G. was far from the first artist to craft such stark crime stories. What sets apart "Niggas Bleed"—and most of B.I.G.'s catalog of story rhymes—was the level of detail and literary craft he employed as a narrator. Beyond the array of adjectives—the gats that are specifically described as stainless steel, the color of the adversary's Range Rover, the number of the motel room where the hustlers were waiting—the song is layered with casual, journalistic observations that give damn-near three-dimensional detail:

Since it's on I called my Nigga Arizona Ron
From Tuscon, pushed a black Yukon
Keeps the slow grooves on—mainly rocks the Isleys
Stupid as a young one, chose not his moves wisely.

In the span of four bars, the artist introduces a new character, tells the listener where that character hails from, what he drives, his affinity for Isley Brothers slow jams, and the fact that he had matured in the game from his days as a buckwild apprentice. As was the custom with the hustlers of old, B.I.G. runs down the man's pedigree, devoting sixteen of the song's forty-eight bars to narrating the background story of Arizona Ron, providing, as it was, his thug resumé. He does the same with Gloria, the in-harms-way manager of the hotel where the score takes place, tipping us that his protagonist (and alter ego), Frank White, had history with her going back years and that his rep was such that she gave up the info he demanded with a quickness.

The telly manager was Puerto Rican
Gloria from Astoria, I went to war

With her peeps—in '91 they stole a gun
From my workers. And they stole drugs
They tried to jerk us.

The hustler's craft is time-refined, aged through the decades of backwater snake-oil dealing and big-city confidence games. Tracks like "Niggas Bleed," as brilliant as they were disturbing, established the MC as the most recent chronicler of that specific layer of human experience. In his definition of literary naturalism, the critic M. H. Abrams proposed that the shared presumption of that movement was that

A person inherits compulsive instincts—especially hunger, the accumulative drive, and sexuality—and is then subject to the social and economic forces in the family, the class, and the milieu into which that person is born.

In hip hop, we find a degree of asphalt naturalism, a literary landscape where characters are motivated by hunger—both physical and metaphorical—and shaped by the unyielding forces of the surrounding world. The battles to be won exist on the level of tangible, material need. From the gate hip hop took as its subject matter the invisible black-brown lives of those dispossessed beings who created it. Ralph Ellison knew of that which he spoke when he placed the unnamed protagonist of *Invisible Man* in an unnamed municipality, painted him black, and then riffed on the nature of epidermal camouflage. At the core of hip hop's being, its rationale for existence, is this refusal to exist as unseen and unseeable. Thus the fact that the word *recognize*—meaning to "identify as previously known, take notice of, acknowledge, especially with appreciation" according to the books—takes a whole 'nother level of connotation within this culture. On this street, to be told to *recognize* is to be issued an injunction, given a warning, schooled to the fact that there are consequences and repercussions for whatever has been said, done, or forgotten. Hip hop is the musical equivalent of Ellison's character deliberately careening into vision-impaired citizens on the street who literally do not know what hit them.

The music journalist Touré broke this dynamic down succinctly when speaking of the thug-icon Tupac Shakur, referring to him as a master performance artist whose canvas is his body, and whose stage is the world. If Tupac escapes jail time, he's the Teflon don, able to leap multiple convictions with a single bound. If he's locked down, he's the realest of the real, going back to his roots (remember, he was in jail as a fetus). Either eventuality carries the bonus of keeping him onstage, which for all its surface political insubstantiality gets at the heart of a very black male necessity: through all the contradictions and posturing and bullshit, it's really about nothing more than never for a single moment being invisible.

But on another level, this is a human concern, not a hip hop–specific one. The story, from the time when the first ancients huddled around the primordial fires, has been the consolation prize for mortality, the assurance that at least one's epic might remain visible to the unborn generations long after you've gone to dust. In precise terms, it means to allow future men to revere you as a hero. And this is a two-way street. The screenwriter and critic Robert McKee points out that

> the world now consumes films, novels, theater and television in such quantities and with such ravenous hunger that the story arts have become humanity's prime source of inspiration, as it seeks to order chaos and gain insight into life. Our appetite for story is a reflection of the profound human need to grasp the patterns of living, not merely as an intellectual exercise, but within a personal, emotional experience. In the words of the playwright Jean Anouilh, "fiction gives life its form."

Things being what they are—and have long been—the stories told within hip hop were often chronicles in which the outlaw and his misdeeds were rendered in verbal neon.

In the years before Satchel's hurricane fastball out-dueled Dizzy Dean's or Joe Louis's fists put Hitler's Aryan propaganda down for the count, black victory lay within the province of myth. For the generations that never witnessed Satchel Paige throwing aspirin tablets past white big leaguers and those who didn't live long enough to see Max Schmeling sprawled like abstract art on the canvas at Madison Square Garden, the quintessential black heroes bore names like Stagolee, the offhanded murderer, and Railroad Bill, the fearless and fearsome locomotive stick-up man.

Earlier I said that if Sonny Liston had not existed, the blues would've had to invent him—and on the real, maybe they already had. That Listonesque Negro made his way through a century of social experience and made himself known again inside hip hop. Both blues and hip hop fix their imagination upon the same kind of raw, unfinished hero in the stories they tell. The blues "Baaad Nigger" is the thematic equivalent of hip hop's "Real Nigga." That explains what the late MC Hood meant on the remix for A Tribe Called Quest's single "Scenario" when he advertised himself as "buckwild like Larry Davis"—the South Bronx hustler who shot six city cops before escaping the City and evading police for weeks. Beneath this is a fundamental concern for the nature of one's existence: audacity, one must recognize, is the antithesis of invisibility.

The historian Lawrence Levine pointed out that this concern with audacity was a consequence of emancipation of a people who had been in a form of bondage that circumscribed every element of one's life.

> The changes that freedom wrought are made particularly clear by focusing on the figures who dominated black lore. The relatively narrow range of secular heroes celebrated by the slaves in their tales underwent considerable transformation in the years of freedom . . . the enduring plight of black Americans produced a continuing need for a folklore that would permit them to express their hostilities and folk heroes whose exploits would allow them to transcend their situation.

The stories told in that folklore, inherited by the blues and bequeathed to hip hop, relay the doings of strong men who, by their brute strength or brute wit, muscle their way beyond the parameters—legal, moral, social, or otherwise—that constrain the rest of us. The hero appears and, by necessity, summons the will to slay dragons—both physical and metaphorical ones—and deliver to us an example of how such problems are to be handled. This is what heroes do.

> Heroism, which is, among other things, another word for self-reliance, is not only the indispensable prerequisite for productive citizenship in an open society; it is also that without which no individual or community can remain free (Albert Murray, *The Hero and the Blues*).

The MC's specific ability to tell the stories of the anonymous city dweller is the contemporary extension of the blues tradition of storytelling and raw street epics created by those migrants whom James Weldon Johnson would've called "the black and unknown bards." Blues is the cornerstone of American popular music, but hip hop is the only one of its progeny to place equal emphasis upon the telling of stories. Thus in hip hop we find the folklore of the twenty-first century.

This is a culture that, on the level of its stylistic temperature, its core principles, right down to the stories it tells about itself, regards one question above other concerns: *who and what does one represent?* In the case of "Niggas Bleed," the tale was told in the first person—deliberately blurring the line between the imaginative creations of Notorious B.I.G., platinum-selling rap artist, and the deadpan confessions of Christopher Wallace, the Catholic-schooled Brooklynite ex-hustler. It would be impossible to understand B.I.G.'s artistic statement without understanding the centrality of his indigenous lands in the Borough of Kings because, dig it or not, the Borough of Kings is the reason for the artistic statement. Same goes for Scarface's battered muse: Houston's notorious Fifth Ward, the Bay Area environs of Freestyle Fellowship, the ATL sprawl that gave rise to the Dungeon Family Collective. And thus, there is no room for fake representation.

By relaying his tale in the first person, the story itself carried greater realism, blazed a more indelible image in the mind of the listener and added to the cocktail of half-facts, overheard truths, and tabloid gospel that composed the artist's own sprawling legend—the way that Hemingway's or Mailer's muscular prose derived credibility from the lives that the writers themselves lived.

Notorious B.I.G. no doubt would've taken it as a compliment that the stark dramatic lines in "Niggas Bleed" could easily be the basis of the first act of a crime movie. MCs, like directors and actors, live and die by their artistic credit limit—the farthest one can stray from "the truth" while still seducing the audience into suspending their disbelief. It might be that hip hop artists are expected to live the tales that they tell because our lives imitate their art and we appreciate reciprocity.

In any case, all autobiographies contain a quotient of fiction if only because memory is imperfect and in saying "I" the MC is speaking for the invisible masses of his own hood. And he is also telling us that his stories are true—even if they never actually happened. Legend proclaims that during his pugilistic prime, Mike Tyson dropped a wad of hundred dollar bills on a crowded dance floor. He then walked over to the bar to drink and glory in his own badness. Then, after hours of booze socializing, he walked to the middle of the floor and casually picked up his still untouched knot of bills on his way out the door. The empirical truth or untruth of the tale is irrelevant—all that matters is that that Tyson's rep remained imposing enough, that it *could be* believed.

The stark realism or anecdotal satire that characterized early hip hop story rhymes was embellished in terms of lyrical structure and rhyme pattern. From the outset, the primary criterion for the MC was his ability to deliver the unforeseen line, the swift double entendre, or use the uncommon word to complete a rhyme phrase. It would take considerable time, however, before artists came to confound the listeners' expectations in terms of the story's structure and dramatic momentum. Where the typical story rhyme, like Slick Rick's "Children's Story" or "La Di Da Di," consisted of a straightforward, beginning-middle-end narration, B.I.G. was among that elite few who broke up that structure, conveying significant portions of the tale via flashbacks. He was also among that small number of MCs who had mastered the verbal plot twist. He ends "Niggas Bleed" with this gem:

> *The funny thing was, through all the excitement*
> *They Range got towed—they double-parked by a hydrant.*

After detailing their reputations for ruthless efficiency throughout the song, we find that they're inept enough to play themselves by walking right past him in the hallway and then leave their car in front of a fire hydrant during a fire. It is a masterstroke of irony. But "Niggas Bleed" wasn't a solitary piece of sublime fiction: that kind of literary flair turned up consistently throughout the man's body of work.

With "Somebody's Gotta Die," the lyrical pulp fiction that appeared with "Niggas Bleed" on B.I.G.'s posthumous double album *Life After Death*, Big provides a Nigga's-eye narration of a hit gone wrong. After being awakened at 3:52 A.M. and hearing that his man C-Rock has just gotten hit up by a one-time partner, Big's first-person character stalks the assailant, letting you know straight up that "retaliation for this one won't be minimal." He takes the time to chastise the un-schooled junior thug who wants to run up into the spot letting off indiscriminate shots:

> *See Niggas like you do ten year bids*
> *Miss the nigga they want and murder innocent kids*
> *Not I. One nigga's in my eye—that's Jason*
> *Ain't no slugs gonna be wasted.*

But if there was any remaining question about the big man's skill as an MC narrator, they dissolve when you realize that the preceding line was the lyrical foreshadowing for the heavy head-trip of an ending he provides four bars later:

> *I get a funny feelin'*
> *Put the mask on in case this nigga start squealin'*
> *Scream his name out, squeeze six, nothin' shorter*
> *The nigga turned around holdin' his daughter*
> *What the fuck?*

In *Story*, McKee also points out that a plot only works when the character is forced to make decisions—and those decisions must have consequences—no matter whether they generate legal drama, loss of love, or a spiritual deficit, but they have to *cost* something. With this cut, the artist hits us with the most ironic of consequences: the revenge-murder that our *hero* has been looking forward to throughout the song becomes the basis of his own moral crisis. Irony is the state of affairs when one's actions achieve precisely the opposite effect of one's intentions. The twist in "Somebody's Gotta Die" lays in the fact that the protagonist created precisely the kind of hood tragedy he had warned his people against—an implicit statement on the stone-cold nature of life, death, and hustle.

On "Warning," from the debut *Ready to Die*, he narrates the conversation between the player and the friend who hips him to the fact that former acquaintances are coming to try to rob his house and "drop his decimals." Where the pedestrian rapper would've laid down a litany of threats that were as unbelievable as they were explicit, B.I.G. was content to issue a masterfully vague understatement:

There's gonna be a lot of slow singing
and flower bringing
if my burglar alarm starts ringing.

Those lines stand as the most chillingly smooth threat this side of Jay-Z's injunction on "Friend or Foe":

You leave me no choice
I leave you no voice
Believe you me son
I hate to do it just as bad
As you hate to see it done.

As in the blues and its ancestral folklore, there are parallel streams in the hip hop story that usually end with the demise of the protagonist or serve to highlight his—and it's almost always *his*—cunning or badness. This latter tendency informs us that the murderer Sheldon "Stack" Lee—the sometime pimp and politician who killed a man for touching his Stetson hat in St. Louis in 1896—was lionized in the epic "Stagolee" not to honor his act of homicide, but because his ornery audacity hinted at a man who was incapable of being compromised—even by a system that had bent the spines of thousands of men who looked like him. In Cecil Brown's perceptive telling:

As an oral performance, Stagolee has influenced a new art form in rap music and hip hop. As an invisible hero, Stagolee is an image of a man who can find dignity in his own country, which seeks to disgrace him . . . Stagolee is anti-myth, the discontinuous, the speech act, and the blues aesthetic. [He] becomes the allegory of the "player," the mack, who never can be destroyed because his existence is conditioned on his not being noticed. Stagolee's story is the secret history extending from the steamboat to the electronic age in the American twenty-first century.

By contrast, the folk tales of Shine, who became the sole survivor of the Titanic disaster by having the good sense to swim home, or the Signifyin' Monkey, whose verbal gamesmanship leads him to outsmart the so-called King of the Jungle, comically highlight the craftiness and wit of the protagonist. These tales, many which have their origins in West African folklore and which were revised and recreated in the context of slavery and segregation, were passed down orally from generation to generation. And given the circumstances under which they were told, it comes as no surprise that a theme of underdog victory is the cornerstone of the tradition. Bad as he undoubtedly was, Stagolee was, in the context of American Jim Crow, an underdog—a fact that makes his audacity all the more impressive.

In hip hop we find the relentless replay of these curbside chronicles and both these streams—the tragic and the near-comic—can be distilled to a common concern: the bruised nature of the world. These tales are often less concerned with conveying a moral than with establishing the bleak consequences of *the Game*—no matter the specific variety of flim-flam that term may refer to—than it is with highlighting the black humor of the well-orchestrated scam. The rendering that you receive is that of a gray and amoral universe where victory is self-justifying, success is a destination, not a journey, and good is quantified by how many numbers precede the decimal point. The stories are peopled by smoked-out slackers, heavy-gunned fugitives, and barrel-bellied cops and are every bit as devoid of complex female life as your classic war flicks.

Given the nature of the lives led in the era in which the blues tales came into existence, the tools of violence (the gun, the shank, and, failing all else, the fist) take exaggerated importance in the their art. Note this line from the blues classic "C.C. Rider":

> *Gon' buy me a shotgun long as I am tall*
> *Gonna buy me a shotgun, long as I am tall*
> *If you don't treat me right*
> *You ain't gonna have no hide at all.*

Or from Skip James's "22–20 Blues":

> *If my baby don't do like I tell her to do*
> *I'll take my 22–20 and cut her half in two.*

Now ponder those references in relation to Ice Cube's "Man's Best Friend," recorded a half-century-plus after Skip James issued his haunting threats.

Here is the reason why Ice Cube pack
Just in case the little punks try to jack
I can't keep a motherfuckin' pit-bull
Under my coat in the small of my back.

Or, for that matter, check Tupac's "Me and My Girlfriend," the metaphorical reference to his *real* constant companion:

Nigga, my girlfriend may be .45
But she still live
One shot making niggas heartbeat stop.

You don't need a press release from the NRA to realize that the gun's standing as the sacred object of the solitary bad man translates neatly from Skip James's tool for relationship mediation over to Tupac's surrogate woman. The gat—and the men who ably wield it—are among the most potent and aged of American symbols. The historian Richard Slotkin points out in *Gunfighter Nation* that

> the "cult of the gunfighter" is constituted by the use of a particular character and style to resolve a wide range of conflicts in a nearly limitless variety of settings. The outward form of the gunfighter style emphasizes artistic professionalism in the use of weapons, but what justifies and directs that professionalism is a particular state of mind, a "gunfighter" understanding of "how the world works." That understanding is essentially "hard-boiled": the world is a hostile place, human motives are rarely good, and outcomes depend not on right but on the proper deployment of might.

We speak here of a place where ministers are murdered on motel balconies in Memphis and the Constitution enshrines one's right to stay strapped.

The rhyme artist Nas riffed on this theme with "I Gave You Power" from the *It Was Written* release, narrating a bitter storyline from the perspective of an aged 9 millimeter pistol that has grown tired of the endless serial drama of the hood. Or, in his phrases, "sick of the blood/sick of the slugs/sick of the wrath for the next man's grudge."

Beyond spinning a masterpiece of hip hop personification, "I Gave You Power"—which could be the literal explanation for accu-

mulated decades of American authority—presented a supreme para-
dox: the lethal weapon that loathes its life of violence, a commentary
on a world so violence-soaked that even its weapons have grown
weary of killing.

> *They pull me out*
> *I watched as Niggas scattered*
> *Making me kill*
> *But what I feel like never mattered.*

In a bit of dramatic irony, the gun begins plotting its owner's demise,
deciding to jam the next time conflict arises. When the hapless thug
pulls the trigger the gun says, "I held on/it felt wrong/knowing niggas
is waiting in hell for him." Predictably the owner is slain and the gun is
momentarily happy—that is, until another thug aspirant grabs him
from the scene of the crime. What Nas accomplished here was more
than a deft piece of writing; "I Gave You Power" was also a commentary on the real implications of the endless reliance upon violence in
both life and art. The cycle begins with death and ends with death and
this saga has replayed itself so many times that even the instruments of
violence bemoan its continuation. Thus, even as some tales of violence
have reached an apex for creative rendering, the theme itself becomes
wearisome.

In hip hop, and the street folklore that informs it, the favored obsession is a particular type of tragic arc: the rise and fall of the hustler-
king. Beneath, above, and beside the posturing that animates hip hop
are the references to the hidden toll exacted by the unforgiving boulevards. In "Somebody Gotta Die," the ending has the protagonist acci-
dentally shooting a child in an attempt to kill the girl's drug-thieving father. Cube's elegiac "Dead Homiez" presents a snapshot of a funeral in
which he lyrically pierces the myth of black male invincibility with the
line

> *They say be strong and your tryin*
> *How strong can you be when you see your pops cryin?*

That same sensibility informed Ice Cube's "Summer Vacation" and
DMX's "Crime Story," bleak tales of wrongs done and the karmic consequences of them—both of which end with death or incarceration of

the protagonist. Jay-Z dedicated an entire song to that reality. "Regrets" appeared, not coincidentally, on his debut, *Reasonable Doubt*—the album released when he was closest, at least in terms of time and lived experience, to the dirt that had gone down in the heart of his native Marcy Projects. Jay-Z was also responsible for the searing lamentation "Meet the Parents," in which a heartless hustler runs the streets from childhood into middle age and winds up unwittingly killing his long-abandoned son in a corner confrontation. Glory, and street glory in particular, are understood as the most fleeting of circumstances. Thus the famed epic of black street lore is titled simply "The Fall." The poem, anonymously and collectively authored, was learned on street corners and in jail cells and passed through the mouths of generations of ghetto initiates. So aptly did it capture the essence of this life that the film director Bill Duke lifted the poem to serve as a type of Shakespearean chorus for his dark-souled cop flick *Deep Cover*.

> *It was Saturday night and the jungle was bright*
> *And the Game was stalking its prey*
> *The code was crime in the neon line*
> *And the weak were doomed to pay.*

The rise:

> *Now I laid and played off the dough she made*
> *From the coast to old Broadway*
> *My game was strong 'cause my money was long*
> *I made this business pay*

But even in his vice glory, the seeds of the inevitable fall are sown:

> *But the trouble began when I ranked my hand*
> *And stopped blowing and started to hit*
> *Why, Jim, you know, I blew all that dough*
> *Faster than any one whore could get.*

> *Then I blew my shack, my Cadillac*
> *My rug up off the floor*
> *I sold my ice at a pawnshop price*
> *And shot up all that dough.*

The tale ends with the bitter moral of a player turned lame:

> *Now here I lay in jail in a six-by-six cell*
> *Watching the sun rise in the East*
> *As the mornings chill the jungle still*
> *I think of that slumbering beast.*

But hip hop was not the first art form to mine these street epics for material. The black pulp novelists Iceberg Slim (né Robert Beck) and Donald Goines created fictional work that mirrored the themes of the older street epics, and their novels in turn midwifed hip hop's narrative sensibilities.

In Iceberg Slim's short story "To Steal a Superfox," a down and out player shoots an impeccable verbal game and wins the allegiance of the most sought-after streetwalker in town. But after winning her favor, he loses her to the hustle itself when a white john kills her. That same theme is precisely echoed by the epic street ballad "Mexicana Rose." This is an anonymous urban toast in which rival players compete for the attentions of a painted Chicana woman. When one prevails, the other, in a fit of jealousy, attempts to kill him. The newly minted concubine willingly takes the bullet for her man, and the player then kills the assailant. In true hood grandiosity, he buries her in all the finery of the material world:

> *I gave her a way-out funeral and didn't spare no cash*
> *I buried her in satin and lace and an ermine sable sash*
> *I gave her the Queen Victoria crown and the Cinderella shoes*
> *And hired Count Basie to play the St. Louis Blues.*

Now compare those two stories to a tale of gangsta love and loss like B.I.G.'s "Me and My Bitch"—where a hustler's woman is slain as a means of striking at the hustler himself—and the narrative lineage connecting folklore, fiction, and hip hop becomes that much more clear.

Iceberg Slim's *Pimp: The Story of My Life* appeared in 1969 and prefaced the wave of street lit that came in the 1970s. Slim's stark, unforgiving urban world was alien to the stylized metropolis of his Tuskegee classmate Ralph Ellison and harsher even than Chester Himes's fictional renderings of Harlem. But like Himes, Iceberg Slim (and Goines after him) began his writing career while incarcerated. Critics declared that Goines "wrote books the way other people package meat," but the realism—advertised even on the level of titles like *Black Gangster, Daddy Cool,* and *Dopefiend*—were the real draw. His work was peopled by velvet-lined pimps, quick-handed hustlers, and ersatz kings and their ghetto courtesans. And the common themes between the two writers was the always-brutal consequences of life on the street.

Both Goines and Iceberg Slim were intimately acquainted with their subject matter. Both men had matriculated through the ranks of the game and shared a common pedigree in the illicit economy. Thus their fiction bore the imprint of authenticity. Their connection to hip hop was as literal as it was literary. The writers were both inheritors and transmitters of a specific genus of cool that the historian Robin D. G. Kelley referred to as the "pimp aesthetic"—an approach to life that has a marrow-deep connection to hip hop as well. Explaining the origins of Miles Davis's enigmatic cool, Kelley wrote

> And while Miles confessed to pimping during his heroin daze, I'm not suggesting that he needed to be a real pimp to embrace the aesthetic. Rather, he was the product of a masculine culture that aspired to be like a pimp, that embraced the cool performative styles of the players (pronounced "playas"), the "macks," the hustlers, who not only circulated in the jazz world but whose walk and talk also drew from the well of black music. Miles's deep distrust of others, his desire for "easy living," his detachment and his violence derive from the same playa principles behind his romanticism, his coolness and sense of style and his incredible storytelling ability.

And you will recall that Malcolm X, the black revolutionary, was built upon the bones of Detroit Red, the uptown pimp whose gilded tongue made the leader as effective at converting blacks to Islam as the player had been at converting women into streetwalkers. Not coincidentally, pimp-esque coolness, style, and verbal ability are central to the hip hop aesthetic. West Coast artists Too Short and Ice-T reflected the most obvious connection to the pimp theme. Ice-T, the MC and one-time pimp, derived his stage name from that of Iceberg Slim. Big Daddy Kane introduced himself to the world with a stage name that befitted a carnal salesman as much as it did a hip hop lyricist. No wonder he complained of the player's occupational hazards on the single "Pimpin' Ain't Easy." (A random sample of hip hop titles would include UGK's "Space-Age Pimpin'," David Banner's "Like A Pimp," 50 Cent's "P.I.M.P.," and Common's "A Film Called Pimp," where he offers the Raymond Chandler-esque observation that "her body language spoke like a smart remark.") Between his debut, *Ready to Die*, and the sophomore release, *Life After Death*, Notorious B.I.G. transformed himself from the unrefined street rep into a platinum polished playa, trading in Timberland boots for tailored suits—pimp couture. And like Goines, who was gunned down by an anonymous assailant in 1974, B.I.G. lived out a death that could've been pulled from the pages of his own gritty fables. Nas borrowed the title for his single "Black Girl Lost" from the 1973 Donald Goines novel of the same name. Nor was it coincidental that Ernest Dickerson's *Never Die Alone*—an adaptation of a Donald Goines novel—starred the rapper DMX. The demise-of-the-fabled hustler theme is a narrative preoccupation connecting all these forms.

Hustler's Convention, the poetic LP released in 1974 by Lightnin' Rod was heavily indebted to that same tradition. Lightnin' Rod was the alias for Last Poet Jalal Nurridin, and under the cloak of his alter-ego he narrated a street tale that was far afield from the revolutionary correctness that defined the Last Poets' content. Constructed in the form of twelve interrelated poems, *Hustler's Convention* is almost a prototype of the brand of storytelling that was central to hip hop three decades later. Any question regarding the significance of *Hustler's Convention* or its connection to hip hop was cleared up by the fact that the Furious Five (after their split with Grandmaster Flash) released an abridged version of the twelve-poem release as a single in 1984 (the poem was covered by at least two other rap artists in subsequent years.)

In hip hop, this reckoning with the tragic bleeds over into a preoccupation with mortality itself. The same spirit that animated Gwendolyn Brooks poem "The Pool Players. Seven At the Golden Shovel"—

We real cool. We
Left school. We

Lurk late. We
Strike straight. We

Sing sin. We
Thin gin. We

Jazz June. We
Die soon.

—is accepted as a common presumption within elements of the music. And like hip hop, Brooks' poem begins with a presumption of cool. The state of affairs is such that the culture delivers these kinds of bitter ironies:

> *Peace to Biggie and Pac*
> *Cause they really were hot*
> *Rap game heavy hitters*
> *It's a shame they no longer with us*

Bear in mind, this is the same artist that wrote

> *I was a gangsta from the get-go*
> *Leavin' fags in body bags with tags on their big toe.*

Both verses appeared on Big L's *Lifestyles of the Poor & Dangerous*—a release that reached shelves shortly before L was gunned down on 139th Street, Harlem, USA.

Like Gabriel García Márquez's short story "Chronicle of a Death Foretold," hip hop narration obsesses over the deaths that are widely known to be imminent in communities that are nonetheless powerless to stop them. Big L, the late Harlem MC, composed songs about the stone-hearted doings on his native 139th Street, his CD art features a photo of the rapper on 139th, and his logo is an image of a man standing on the corner under the 139th Street sign. In short, L gave the world an image of the rapper as boulevard boss, a man posted up on avenue with the mandate to rep hard or go home. His work was defined by a limited palette of themes; he offered up permutations of bitches, guns, and income as subject matter. But the local allegiances were clear. And it was in that same locale that the artist was fatally shot in the face over an ephemeral beef of ambiguous origins.

A culture, in order to qualify as such, must render some element of life more intelligible. Human experience is bound together by the experiences of birth, maturation, love, sex, procreation, and death, but it is the existence of culture that makes sense of these phenomena. Were we to create a catalog of hip hop music since its inception, we would find the themes of sex (often distilled down to its mechanical basics) and death to be vastly overrepresented. Whereas the blues certainly acknowledges the reality of death, it chooses to focus on the pain of love that has reached its expiration date. Hip hop, however, has a deeply ambivalent perspective on romantic attachment. (It has, coincidentally, a far easier time expressing fraternal love as typified by Tupac's ode "When My Homiez Call" on the album *Strictly For My N.I.G.G.A.Z.* and 50 Cent's declaration that "There ain't shit in this life deeper than loyalty and love/except loyalty and love between thugs.") Like the martial arts flicks of old, the music is shot through with the theme of risking one's life to avenge the death of a male comrade, but rare is the reference to doing the same to defend the honor of one's woman.

At the heart of this tendency is the fact that much of hip hop has been created by men who are under the age of twenty-five. Hip hop is literally the youngest form of African American music. The blues singer, the jazz musician, and the soul singer have the luxury of maturing and grappling with the idea of romantic love in more complex ways. Yet we see hip hop showing its age—or immaturity—in the common adolescent conflation of love, loss, and heartbreak with weakness. And the culture from which hip hop was spawned can tolerate anything but weakness. The niche-marketed nature of the music industry ensured that hip hop would age, while not necessarily maturing. More often than not, the twenty-year-old artist who emerged in 1994 rapping for an audience of his peers finds himself a decade later rapping for an audience the age of his nephews or younger brothers. The result is a kind of prolonged adolescence when it comes to matters of emotional attachment to females.

Thus it is death, not love, that is on hip hop's mind. This is a morose perspective, but it is also rooted in statistical truth. Hip hop was created in large part by the segment of society that is most likely to die violently. Thus in hip hop, we witness the ongoing attempt to come to terms with needless mortality—a reality that defines the communities from which the culture sprung. Thus for an artist like Scarface, witnessing death becomes as prominent an artistic theme as it was in Edgar Allan Poe's death-haunted fiction. Bear in mind that this is the same music in which B.I.G. and Tupac Shakur were hailed as prescient for creating lyrical content that in some ways foreshadowed their own passing to the other side. And this reckoning is at turns resolved and ambivalent (note early Nas stating that "When its my time to go/I'll wait for god with the 4-4," or 50 Cent's declaration that he keeps heat in his waist in the event that God fails him). But the heretical truth is that the claims to prescience fall flat in the face of facts. These are chronicles of deaths foretold in epics of the ancestors. Gwendolyn Brooks's poem begins with the statement of cool and ends with the reckoning of premature death. *We Die Soon.* The distinction now is that now not even the teller of the tale is immune to the bitter end of the story.

BOULEVARD NOIR

No matter how deep hip hop's roots in the black storytelling tradition, it would be dead wrong to believe that the music was hermetically sealed in a racial sub-basement of America. Even as it was birthed from the specific traditions of black folklore, it developed in dialogue with America at-large—specifically the cinematic traditions of noir and gangster films. This relationship was obvious as far back as the Golden Era when Rakim, who was, as always, ahead of the curve, presented the video for "Follow the Leader" in which the MC and his sonic sideman Eric B. were re-imagined as 40s-era gangsters.

> *I watch a gangsta flick and root for the bad guy*
> *Turn it off before the end because the bad guy dies.*
> —*50 Cent*

Were it not for the white noise of criticism surrounding the art form, it would have been recognized long ago that the tales narrated in hip hop are also the latest installment in the tradition of American pulp. The hip hop narrative is the unrequited step-child of the American crime epic; the music takes as its primary concerns those same themes expressed in this country's primordial folklore, the themes projected onto screens of the mind by Coppola, Scorsese, and De Palma, and penned by Marlowe, Chandler, and Spillane.

And this is, at its most elemental core, an American dialogue. The obsessive concern with violence that permeates hip hop—and the understanding of it as fundamental aspect of masculinity—descends only partly from the specific history of black people in the United States. Hip hop springs from the blues-folklore and street epic poetry of the Great Migration; but truth told, a textbook revenge-murder tale like Nas's

"The Set Up" has to be understood as being as much a product of the tradition of American pulp fiction and gangland cinema as it is anything that coalesced in his native hood of Queensbridge.

The fingerprint details of hip hop—the gun as icon, the jaundice-eyed perspective on the world, the muscularity of the language, the centrality of the City as a backdrop, the endless replay of the woman-as-Eve theme, and the all-consuming pursuit of the dollar—descend from the fictional worlds of Sam Spade and Philip Marlowe, the cinematic environs of Don Corleone and *Goodfellas*. Think about that in the context of Obie Trice's "The Set Up" (not to be confused with Nas's song of the same title) or Common's "Testify," two songs in which male protagonists are cleverly undone by beautiful but treacherous women, and it's hard to miss the similarity between those tales and the standard noir formula. "The Set Up" relays the story of a woman who organizes a drug heist only to double-cross her own team and see to it that both sides are robbed. On that same score, Raymond Chandler's short story "Goldfish" centers on a murder committed during a jewel heist. The assailant turns out to be not any of the hardened thieves who specialize in such activities, but rather the delicate-faced young woman, whose beauty belied her stone cold disposition.

In hip hop, as in the gangster flick, we witness the spectrum of emotion telescoped down to the poles of anger and cool and character motivation driven by greed or loyalty. It is no coincidence that Tony Montana, Al Pacino's cocaine-addled Horatio Alger in the cult gangster flick *Scarface*, has become the patron saint of the MC. Hip hop is Jimmy Cagney shouting out his mama from the top of the world. It is Scarface' coke-fueled rage before literally blowing up and falling off, Nino Brown (Wesley Snipes's cinematic stand-in for Harlem heroin king Nicky Barnes) shot through the heart and going over the balcony in *New Jack City*.

The gangster is a particularly American product. This country did not invent crime, but the gangster's stylized aesthetic version of villainy is native to this soil. And that understanding of violence—both real and implied—as a form of beauty is impossible to understand outside the influence of American cinema. To cut to the quick, John Gotti, the silver-haired, custom-fitted don and 80s era media reference owed his existence in equal parts to the gangster Lucky Luciano and the actor Edward G. Robinson. The vision of the gangster as a wisdom-dispensing CEO of the underworld was crafted and refined by Mario Puzo's novel *The Godfather* and delivered to the American masses by Coppola's screen adaption. That stylized version of organized crime was deliberately turned on its head in *Goodfellas*, whose "made men" inhabit a grey, amoral, ill-tailored world where violence looks violent. But myths cannot flourish in the face of that kind of cinematic journalism. And that explains why Don Corleone, not Henry Hill, has remained the default setting in our imagination of the mob boss, not only in hip hop, but in America at large. Still, the cinematic and gangster references within the genre are innumerable and inseparable. Christopher Wallace, in fact, copped his mic alias Biggie Smalls from Calvin Lockhart's gangster character in the con-man comedy *Let's Do It Again*. Foxy Brown took her name from the heroine of Pam Grier's 1974 blaxploitation flick. Truth told, the Queens-born MC Kiam Holley would have no basis for calling himself "Capone" had the real-life gangster not been enshrined in American mythology by film—and bestowed the posthumous honor of being portrayed by Robert De Niro. The Houston-based lyricist who was born as Brad Johnson made his professional debut as Scarface, taken directly from the title of Brian De Palma's 1983 remake of the 1932 gangster classic. Arguably the most influential film within the genre, *Scarface* had for the hip hop generation the same resonance that *Easy Rider* held for the disaffected white youth of 1970s America or *Sweet Sweetback's Baadasssss Song* had for black men in the Black Power era.

In *Scarface*, hip hop lyricists found a protagonist cut from their own cloth, the low-end player who amplifies his hustle to kingpin status. The tragic arc of the film's hero met the expectations of a generation who had learned that success has mortal costs from generations of urban folklore, fiction, and lived experience. So this was not fatalism; this was a blank-faced recognition that in business as in war, death is the price for glory. Look closer at hip hop's fascination with the gangster and what you recognize is a stained and battered allegiance to the American dream. Zora Neale Hurston once wrote that the poor Negro is the most fervent subscriber to the dream of American Becoming—a faith immune to the social exile of Jim Crow and the long-shot odds of economic mobility. The song describing the deprivations of the past and highlighting one's present financial largeness is so common within hip hop as to be a cliché. But in that same vein, the grandiosity and flamboyant materialism is not solely a product of the *nouveau riche*, or, in the hip hop terminology, the *ghetto fabulous*. In the era of mob boss John Gotti, it became apparent that the same degree of comic foppishness and style was seen in the real-life gangsters seeking to emulate the cinematic depictions of their professional attire. If capitalism is the American religion, then the gangster is a rough-hewn altar boy. And on that level, hip hop is American as a motherfucker.

BEARING WITNESS: (AUDIOBIOGRAPHY)

While the tale of how we suffer and how we are delighted, and how we may triumph is never new, it must always be heard. There isn't any other to tell, it's the only light we've got in all this darkness . . . and this tale, according to that face, that body, those strong hands has a new depth in every generation.

—James Baldwin

You will know the truth when it is spoken and it will change you. This was an axiom of faith among the chattel and those free beings whom they begat. The dated observation that the "personal is political" has gone threadbare from repetition, but that does nothing to diminish the truth of that cliché. And truth is what is at issue here. This reality drove Oloudah Equiano, Harriet Jacobs, Frederick Douglass, and those once-slaves who started the tradition of black autobiography. It was known by those Sunday morning testifiers of the black church, who fashioned their individual stories into an amicus brief in the court of the Lord. It was long ago recognized that autobiography among the ignored is an act of self-salvation. Thus, the telling of one's life story on these shores began with the explicit purpose of delivering the extended clan from the degradation of bondage. (In that same tradition, Richard Wright offered himself as a witness for the prosecution with *Black Boy* and its exposé of the manifold evils of segregation a century later.) At the root is this simple and profound assertion: if one has a story, then they must, in fact, *exist*. As full human beings. Contrary to whatever social mythology and fractional legal compromises would have you believe.

Dwell with that thought for a moment.

Now consider hip hop as an extension not only of the black musical tradition on these shores, but the autobiographical one as well.

Listen for a moment to Pete Rock and CL Smooth's "They Reminisce Over You (T.R.O.Y.)" and it will deliver to you nostalgia for a life that you never lived and recollections of memories that are not yours. Dedicated to Trouble T-Roy, the recently deceased friend of the vocalist,

"Reminisce" is a snapshot of a young man coming to understand himself as part of a lineage, a genealogy not of flat caricatures and shaded-in stereotypes, but of three-dimensional human beings whose lives have shaped his own. Men and women with breadth, width, and depth who are his family. We hear him narrate his own birth to an eighteen-year-old single mother:

> Count all the fingers and the toes
> Now I suppose you hope the little black boy grows.

And speak of the grandfather who stepped into the paternal role:

> Took me from a boy to a man so I always had a father
> When my biological didn't bother.

By the song's conclusion you know of his younger sister's birth, his mother's marriage after ten years of single parenthood, the friend who believed in his talent—"Only you saw what took many time to see"—and you feel the sting of that premature loss.

At its most fertile and fragile moments, when bullshit was suspended and truth given license, hip hop was a means by which a new generation could render their own lives in their full three dimensions. To give evidence of deals that must be cut every day, in the words of Talib Kweli, *just to get by*. That tradition dated back to the earliest stages of hip hop's evolution. Part of the effectiveness of Melle Mel's searing verses on "The Message" lay in the fact that they were told in the first person—and the listener was left wondering where the artist's lyrical journalism ended and the autobiographical confessions began.

With their 1994 single "C.R.E.A.M. (Cash Rules Everything Around Me)," the newly debuted Wu-Tang Clan provided what would be the high water mark for self-reflection from their collective—with the exception of some of Ghostface Killah's more raw revelations on *Iron Man*. But from the opening lines, "I grew up on the crime side, the *New York Times* side/staying alive was no jive," "C.R.E.A.M." was another level of self-expression, telling of the vicious cycle of street life from naiveté, to initiation in the drug hustle, to incarceration, to the futile attempt to convey a warning to the next generation of would-be hustlers: "Shorty's running wild, smoking ces, drinking beer/and ain't tryin to hear what I'm kickin' in his ear."

The most tangible connection between these two streams of autobi-ography is Malcolm X's searing tale of a hustler's salvation. Reaching shelves in 1965, *The Autobiography of Malcolm X* echoed through the mouths of later writers who wrote of the treacherous paths of black male becoming. Malcolm's narrative informed Piri Thomas's *Down These Mean Streets,* Huey P. Newton's *Revolutionary Suicide,* and came all the way down to Cody Scott's *Monster* and Nathan McCall's *Makes Me Wanna Holler.* In life, Malcolm was a rarity. Fused in him was an incisive intellect, an ascetic's discipline, and a hustler's spirit. A succession of en-vironments in which young Malcolm Little was not so much raised as brought to a boil gave birth to his new incarnation, Detroit Red, the up-town player. Hard prison time and Elijah Muhammad's teachings made him into Malcolm X, and he made himself El-Hajj Malik El-Shabazz, but he never entirely shook free of Detroit Red, the street initiate who under-stood all the angles. And that fact alone explains why Malcolm became such a revered icon to the hip-hop generation in the late 1980s.

In the 90s, an era in which black leadership's greed, polyester, and li-bido invalidated whatever words fell from their mouths, the long-de-ceased Malcolm attained a standing that was nearly unimpeachable. Piece together the snippets of his speeches jacked from aged recordings and dropped into hip hop songs and you could construct an anthology of his most important work. And this reverence was not isolated among hip hop's political vanguard, your Chuck Ds and KRS-Ones. In legend and in life, his epic resonated among varied slices of black life. Whether by in-tention, coincidence, or the unchanging nature of life on the south side of town, the autobiographical songs in hip hop echo the life story that Mal-colm relayed to Alex Haley in the months before his premature end.

The basic format of the autobiography in general is to relay one's journey through difficult experience and the hard-gleaned wisdom re-ceived in the process. But Malcolm and the later generation of MCs shared more than a basic format. Malcolm exists as both the ancestral hustler and the wise man who rose above the streets while never aban-doning them. And thus, the trajectory of his life—birth, the dissolution of his family, the experience of poverty and beginning of his life as a hustler, his incarceration, and his eventual redemption—is played out endlessly within hip hop.

It would be an oversimplification to say that the Malcolm X formula explains the entirety of hip hop autobiography, even as his life contains great similarities to those life stories told within the music. The genre also contains autobiographical songs like Lauryn Hill's willfully nostalgic "Every Ghetto, Every City," Andre 3000's free-association narration "A Life in the Day," and Jean Grae's "Love Song," which chronicles her painfully learned lessons on the nature of love. (She brilliantly details the rise and fall of a three-year relationship using the pronouns *he, she,* and *they* before confessing "it's easier to talk about this shit in third person.") Still, it is impossible not to notice the similarity between the life that Malcolm detailed in the pages of his book and those that are commonly spoken of in hip hop.

The first sentence of Malcolm's autobiography informs us that "When my mother was pregnant with me, she told me later, a party of hooded Ku Klux Klan riders galloped up to our home in Omaha, Nebraska." Within the first pages, we learn of the dissolution of his family and the brutal death his father met on the railroad tracks of Lansing, Michigan. His father's absence is the result either of a racist murder or accidental tragedy, but the reality of fatherlessness impacts Malcolm nonetheless. In his father's absence, the once-stable family begins a debilitating slide into poverty.

> In late 1934, I would guess, something began to happen. Some kind of psychological deterioration hit our family circle and began to eat away at our pride. Perhaps it was the tangible evidence that we were destitute. . . . I began to drop in about dinnertime at the home of some family that we knew. I knew that they knew exactly why I was there, but they never embarrassed me by letting on. They would invite me to stay for dinner and I would stuff myself.

Now think of that in the context of the later autobiographical songs in hip hop where fatherlessness and poverty are the two most prevalent themes. Check Obie Trice's narration of his own birth on "Follow My Life":

> *Mama ain't breast feed*
> *Had no pop need*
> *He ain't leave shit but a name—Obie.*

In that same vein, DMX's single "Slippin" raises the question

> *Was it my fault, somethin' I did*
> *To make a father leave his first kid—at Seven?*

That same sentiment is echoed on Ghostface Killah's "All I Got Is You" when he says,

> *Sadly, Daddy left me at the age of six*
> *I didn't know nothin.' Mommy neatly packed his shit.*

Treach, the lead rapper of Naughty By Nature, issued the autobiographical "Ghetto Bastard" on their debut *19 Naughty III*, where he states in boldfaced hostility:

> *I was one who never had, was always mad*
> *Never knew my dad, motherfuck the fag.*

Jay-Z, who, with the exception of Tupac Shakur, has arguably inscribed more of his personal biography into his music than any of his contemporaries, deals with this same theme on "Moment of Clarity" from *The Black Album*. But where the father's absence is often a source for venomous anger, "Moment of Clarity" finds the artist contemplative following the death of his long-absent father.

> *So Pop I forgive you*
> *For all the shit that I lived through*
> *It wasn't all your fault*
> *Homie, you got caught.*

Still, that paternal absence has material consequences. On "C.R.E.A.M.," Raekwon rhymes,

> *I had second-hands*
> *Mom bounced on old man*
> *So then we moved to Shao-Lin Land.*

Wu-Tang member Ghostface Killah describes living in a three-room apartment with fifteen residents and "picking roaches out the cereal box" before having breakfast as a child.

As with the deprivations in Malcolm's young life, poverty is the surest path into the illicit economy, a world with its own order of hierarchy, codes of conduct, and principles. Jay-Z spoke of the crack trade as being addictive not only to the fiends who consume the product, but also to the quicker-than-the-law hustlers who get high on the danger, style, reverence, and money that are products of the trade. In his time, the young Malcolm was nearly hypnotized by the neon glow of 1940s-era Harlem and the ad hoc bands of players who inhabited nearly every corner. He recalled his introduction to the ways of uptown as such:

> The pimps would sidle up close, stage-whispering, "All kinds of women, Jack—want a white woman?" And the hustlers were merchandising: "Hundred dollar ring, man, diamond; ninety-dollar watch, too—look at 'em. Take 'em both for twenty-five." In another two years I could've given them all lessons . . . on that night I had started on my way to becoming a Harlemite. I was going to become one of the most depraved parasitical hustlers among New York's eight · million people.

In hip hop, you find serial plays of the story of the adolescent male, too unruly to remain at home, being turned out and initiated into the hustling life. On "Don't Come Down" Obie Trice recalls being thrown out as an adolescent and moving to sell crack rocks: "locks changed and the nights got colder . . . I'm slinging boulders." On UGK's "One Day," from their *Ridin Dirty* release, Pimp C lyricizes:

> *Mama put me out at only fourteen*
> *So I start selling crack cocaine and codeine.*

Treach informed his listeners that

> *I couldn't get a job, nappy hair was not allowed*
> *My mother couldn't afford us all so she had to throw me out.*

That turn of events set his life on the streets in motion:

> *I got laughed at, I got chumped, I got dissed*
> *I got upset, I got a tech and a banana clip.*

Big Boi of OutKast relays a similar story on the autobiographical "West Savannah":

> *My mama had a nigga at the age of 15*
> *My daddy was sellin that sack now he gots responsibilities.*

The young MC later, we hear, follows in his father's footsteps, slinging in the projects. Though the craft requires keeping a "nine in my hand, an ounce in my crotch," the risks provide lucrative rewards: "the money I make be putting cable in every room."

But the hustler's life is one in which freedom is nearly always a temporary state of affairs. For those in "the life," incarceration is a certainty—as sure as death, taxes, and racism in America. Malcolm speaks of his imprisonment in *The Autobiography*, noting the devolution of his character once locked away:

> I preferred the solitary that this behavior brought me. I would pace for hours like a caged leopard, viciously cursing aloud to myself. And my favorite targets were the bible and God. But there was a legal limit to how much time one could be kept in solitary. Eventually, the men in the cellblock had a name for me: "Satan." Because of my antireligious attitude.

UGK's "One Day" covered this same bend in the road, saying, "The only thing promised to a player is the penitentiary." Inspectah Deck narrates his own path to incarceration on "C.R.E.A.M.":

> *A man with a dream with plans to make cream*
> *With failed. I went to jail at the age of fifteen.*

Notorious B.I.G. speaks of his incarceration as a theme on *Ready To Die*, an experience summed up by his words:

> *Rap was secondary, money was necessary*
> *Until I got incarcerated—kinda scary*
> *C74-mark 8 set me straight*
> *Not able to move behind the great steel gate.*

And like Malcolm, these stories culminate in the pursuit of a new (legal) craft in which the skills that had been honed in the hustle become assets. The historian Robin D. G. Kelley has written that Malcolm the revolutionary was formed and informed by the life of Malcolm the uptown hustler. And Malcolm himself understood that the verbal game he had polished during his days as a pimp serviced Elijah Muhammad's crusade to redeem black souls. The MC speaks of the street-informed skills that allow for success within the music industry. But unlike Malcolm's story, where redemption entails opposition to the system that destroyed his family and lay a twisted path before him, hip hop's version of redemption invariably end with success on those very same terms. This was apparent from the time the twenty-year-old Nas opined on the hallmark *Illmatic* that "somehow this rap game reminds me of the crack game." In hip hop, the goal is less about opposition to the system than it is about moving swiftly through the legit channels available within that system. That was the meaning behind Jay-Z's irony-laced decision to name his company Roc-A-Fella records (a play on the term "rock" as avenue shorthand for crack cocaine and the surname for the nineteenth-century robber baron). He expounded on that theme on "Rap Game/Crack Game" from the autobiographical release *In My Lifetime, Vol. I* with lines like:

> We treat this rap shit just like handling weight
> What they want, we give it to 'em. What they abandon, we take.

On "C.R.E.A.M.,"Inspectah Deck ends his bitter tale of youthful crime and incarceration with a reference to his life knowledge he is now in a position to deliver to adolescents confronting the same circumstances that he once had:

> Leave it up to me while I be living proof
> And kick the truth to the young black youth.

As with maternal disappointment, redemption holds particular significance in the eyes of the mother. Obie Trice's "Don't Come Down" is simultaneously an autobiography and an apology to his mother (the song's hook is punctuated by the words "I'm sorry" and begins with the words "As a child I was foul"). The song chronicles his early life and his movement into the drug trade as his mother drove in tears past the corner where he hustled cocaine. It culminates with him informing his mother that the life skills she taught him had kept him from being killed on the streets and made the basis for his success as a rap artist: "You're the reason when I hustled, I knew to stack/when I opened up mics I knew to rip." He ends telling her to look at her son:

> *When they ask about your boy you don't put your head down*
> *Straighten up ma, you can smile now proud.*

Similarly, Goodie Mob's "Guess Who," from the debut *Soul Food*, is a lyrical apology to the artists' mothers:

> *It still amaze me*
> *The lord had to help her raise me*
> *Judging from how I used to be.*

Ghostface Killah's "All I Got Is You" is dedicated to his mother for enduring the struggles in raising him. Jay-Z's "You Must Love Me" witnesses the artist seeking redemption for the unfathomable sins committed against his family during his time as a hustler:

> *Since the date of my birth*
> *All I gave you was hurt.*

Malcolm's time did not favor him with redemption in the eyes of his mother, who was committed to an insane asylum, though he did inform Alex Haley that

> I have rarely talked to anyone about my mother, for I believe that I am capable of killing a person, without hesitation, who happened to make the wrong kind of remark about my mother.

At the very least, that dialogue between Malcolm and his descendants gives the lie to the hollow dismissals of the music as unrelated to any previous form of black expression. Multiply Malcolm by four decades of ensuing history and add a breakbeat. The result would be an autobiography measured in percussion, not pages. However it might be termed, the hip hop autobiography, like its ancestral forms, is concerned with a brand of emancipation and deliverance not from bondage, but from the same kind of American dead end that birthed Detroit Red. Stripped down to its barest components, the autobiography is the attempt of a singular individual to make sense of their time. One might consider a life as a collection of days with a theme, and the fortunate souls come to understand that theme before the final credits roll. The telling of one's tale is a human rite. And in the end, we are simply the stories we tell.

5

Seven MCs

Every legend, moreover, contains its residuum of truth, and the root
function of language is to control the universe by describing it.

—James Baldwin

RAKIM: 360 DEGREES IN THE SHADE

I take seven MCs, put 'em in a line. Speak these nine words to a true listener and see what happens. There are a handful of lines that have
blazed their way into the collective memory and become shorthand for
the works that contained them. It would be impossible, at this point, to
separate *The Godfather* from *I made him an offer he couldn't refuse* or *White
Heat* from *Made it, Ma, the top of the world*. Rakim delivered that to hip
hop with a single 12" released in 1986. "Eric B. Is President" and its b-
side, "Check Out My Melody," heralded the arrival of a whole 'nother
approach to the form, so radical a disjuncture with what had come before it that it could literally make your head hurt thinking about it.
Doubt that if you wish. But repeat to any true hip hop head the nine ital-
icized words at the beginning of this paragraph and see what happens.
The response, coming like an involuntary reflex or part of a religious
catechism will be: *Then add seven more brothers who think they can rhyme.*

There is an indelible whistle that heralds the beginning of the track,
like the preamble to great oration. Then come the scratches, the handi-
work of Eric B., the DJ and producer. And then comes the voice. Nearly
two decades after "Check Out My Melody" first vibrated out of a set a
speakers, Rakim remains the standard by which MCs are measured. In
order to catch the magnitude of what Rakim did that summer in 1986,
you would have to recognize what and where hip hop was prior to his
arrival. Run DMC, Whodini, and LL had become the dominant voices
within the music, sweeping away the Old School and inaugurating the

Golden Era of hip hop. The vocabulary and lyrical complexity of the newer artists was greater than that of the preceding generation, but nowhere near what Rakim introduced to the genre. With Ra, the sound, the rumbling, thunder-of-god baritone, the gleaming sharpness of the style, and the impossible slickness of his flow made it seem as if the preceding decade of hip hop lyricism either did not exist or he had simply stepped outside of that particular history. Unlike LL or Run DMC, Rakim was too blasé to bother raising his voice, much less his pulse rate on the microphone. Where LL's remix for "Rock the Bells" was the definition of lyrical fury, Ra crafted the aesthetic of effortlessness, sounding relaxed, almost somnolent on the microphone. It was an effect that would have damned any other MC with the label *boring*. Instead, it was hypnotic. An entire lineage of MCs took notes when Rakim announced, in typically casual cadence, "This is how it should be done."

His style was identical to none. But that didn't mean that there would not be imitators. If imitation was the sincerest form of flattery, then Rakim might be the most complimented artist of that entire era. He predicted as much on the single "I Ain't No Joke" when he charged that MCs would

> *Put my tape on pause and add more to yours*
> *Then you figure you're ready for the neighborhood chores.*

At the very least, the deliberate rhyme lethargy of fellow Long Islanders EPMD and the bass rumblings of King Sun were products of the post-Rakim era. *Paid In Full*, the debut LP released the following year, was an instant classic. By later standards, it was short—containing only eight songs and two instrumental tracks. But inside the space of those eight tracks—each of them a down payment for a greatest hits collection—the magnitude of the challenge he laid down became clear. Any of those tracks might've justified classic status; singles like "I Ain't No Joke," "Move the Crowd," and "I Know You Got Soul" had hip hoppers believing they'd seen our equivalent of *Bitches Brew*. Where the pace of flow was speeding up, Ra dragged the flow down to a drawl. Where the demands of hip hop's increasing commercialization required radio-friendly, accessible hits, Ra crafted layered metaphors and triple entendres. None of his peers—or successors for that matter—ever succeeded in packing equal density of meaning into a simple sentence: "I hold the microphone like a grudge" or "If I was water, I'd flow in the Nile," or

"On this journey, you're the journal, I'm the journalist," or the classic "When I die bury my rhyme books in Cairo." Part of his advantage came from his musical lineage. In the days before adopting the teachings of the 5% Nation, which had been founded by the Harlem mystic Clarence 13X, the young William Michael Griffin had studied the saxophone. His older brother played piano, his mother sang jazz, and his aunt is the R&B legend Ruth Brown. When he put down the sax and picked up the microphone, the knowledge of chords, timing, and rhythm became the basis for his approach to rhyming. His conversion and adoption of the name Rakim at age sixteen gave him the material that would become a defining element of his music.

He told you from the earliest that he was God. On some level it made sense: if God was from Long Island and had a taste for ripping microphones, he would sound like Rakim. But his self-deification came from his 5% teachings, which held that all black men were gods. His records became the forum in which he expounded on the theology of the 5% Nation that informed later acts like Poor Righteous Teachers, Brand Nubian, and the Wu-Tang Clan, but Rakim was its foremost articulator bar none. Listen to his more abstract verses like

3/4th of water make seven seas
a third of land, 3–60 degrees.

and you get a window into kind of esoterica he was lacing into hip hop.

The single "In the Ghetto" from the *Let the Rhythm Hit 'Em* LP begins with statement "Planet Earth is my place of birth," as if he was bent on clearing up suspicions that the god was from elsewhere in the galaxy. Outside the astrological references of the 5%ers, he dilated the possibilities of the music, musing about travel to the outer edges of the universe and the inner depths of the mind. (Classic Rakim threatened to push a rival's eyeballs "waay into the back of his head" so he could see what he was getting into—"a part of the mind he never been to.") Aside from Kool Keith of the Ultra Magnetic MCs, Rakim was alone in incorporating that kind of sci-fi abstraction into a music that had previously been mired in the material realities of the world. That approach went all the way down to his double entendre of a name. Rakim Allah, or Ra, also recalled the named of the sun god of the ancient Egyptian tradition.

Where most artists had fans, Rakim was getting acolytes. But at the same time, it's not hard to believe that Rakim was becoming a victim of his own profundity. Outside the five boroughs, where audiences had a base knowledge of 5% mysticism, listeners who might be baptized by his unearthly flow were still left wondering what exactly he was talking about. That did not mean that he was without commercial appeal—literally. The core of his audience overlooked his dalliance with the market in the early 90s when he recorded two commercials for St. Ides Malt Liquor—a contradiction to his image as hip hop's devout seeker of wisdom.

But other commercial undertakings were less contradictory and ultimately more memorable. Ex-Shalimar vocalist Jody Watley tapped the Ra to collaborate on her single "Friends" in 1989. While Melle Mel's contribution to Chaka Khan's "I Feel For You" was almost a studio gimmick, Ra's baritone versifying *made* "Friends." He was largely responsible for the re-arrangement of the basic structure of R&B songs in the 1990s. After "Friends" it was more or less *expected* that an R&B song would contain a sixteen-bar rap in its center. The innumerable rapper-singer collaborations that followed had no idea how deeply indebted they were to the self-professed god from Long Island, New York. (For those lacking in long-term memory, Ra returned to form in 2002, dropping sixteen blazing bars onto "Addictive," the collaboration with R&B singer Truth Hurts.)

On the heels of *Paid in Full*, Eric B. & Rakim delivered a full clip of an album titled *Follow the Leader* in 1988. Featuring a broader spectrum of sounds than the James Brown samples that had defined the initial release, *Follow the Leader* saw Rakim at his most lyrically fierce, issuing deft and def threats on such tracks as "Microphone Fiend," "Lyrics of Fury," and the nearly felonious "No Competition." The release marked the high point in the collaboration between the two and prefaced the long slide that they faced in the 1990s. Neither *Let the Rhythm Hit 'Em* nor *Don't Sweat the Technique* reached the level of commercial or critical acclaim that the first two releases had. By the mid 90s, blasphemers were beginning to wonder aloud if the god had clay feet.

It'll take seven more before I go for mine . . .

Illmatic was delivered seven years after *Paid in Full* had redefined the art of MCing. Nas, the poetic sage of the Queensbridge projects, was hailed as the second coming of Rakim—as if the first had reached his expiration date. In the lifespan of a culture, seven years is not a long time, but in popular music—and especially in hip hop—it is a millennium. Virtually none of the class of 87–88—Chuck D, Biz-Markie, Big Daddy Kane, Kool G. Rap, even LL Cool J—was a driving force in the music by 1994. But Rakim, along with KRS-One, had attained a standing that by that point remained unimpeachable. The point was not that Nas was hailed as "the next Rakim," but that Rakim was still the man to whom a vast new talent would necessarily be compared.

Nas never became "the next Rakim," nor did he really have to. *Illmatic* stood on its own terms. The sublime lyricism of the CD, combined with the fact that it was delivered into the crucible of the boiling East-West conflict, quickly solidified the younger artist's reputation as the premier writer of his time. Complicating matters, Rakim completed an album that was easily on par with his earlier work, but contractual disputes prevented it from being released. The result was that the dominant lyricist of the 1980s was left mute for the better part of the 1990s. *The 18th Letter,* Rakim's sixth LP, was released in 1997 and reminded the hip hop audience of precisely what they had missed in his absence, but an even longer quiet spell followed that offering.

In the meantime, Ra had aged into the closest thing the music had to an elder statesman, collaborating with younger artists like Mobb Deep. He turned in the uninspired "R.A.K.I.M." on the *8 Mile* soundtrack after scorching both Dr. Dre and Jay-Z on "The Watcher" from Jay-Z's *The Blueprint*[2] album. Twenty years after the 12" "Eric B. for President" reached stores, the artist's reverberations can still be felt within the music—a claim that none but a small few could make with a straight face. His claim to that position was substantiated by the fact that in hip hop, an arena where patricide is considered an art form, Nas crafted an homage titled "Unauthorized Biography of Rakim" on his 2005 *Street's Disciple* release. Rakim was not a perfect MC—his defenders tend to overlook his deficits as a storyteller. Nor was he a particularly adventurous artist. His style was inexplicably complex in its simplicity, but not unpredictable. He had flow that was intricate, not elaborate. But the individual parts added up to something that might not be matched in the music. Or at least until the god chooses to bless a mic once more.

LAURYN HILL: OLD SOUL MUSIC

You don't have to re-skim that college-worn copy of *Invisible Man* to recognize that the world is hard on black prodigies. For that gem of wisdom, you need only observe the sine curve of Lauryn Hill's career. The artist who left your head spinning with her debut, *The Miseducation of Lauryn Hill*, is long gone. But then, so is the you that first heard it.

There are unassailable truths, like all multiples of nine eventually adding up to nine, that left-handed people die earlier, and that Lauryn Hill, at the time of her debut, was the oldest soul ever seen enshrined in a twenty-three-year-old body. And we suspected this truth since we heard her bear vocal witness on the Fugees' undernourished debut, *Blunted on Reality*. We had an inkling when she used the word *puerile* in a rhyme—swiftly, not sounding like she'd just befriended the word. But you knew it like your address, like part of your personal canon of facts the first time you heard *The Miseducation of Lauryn Hill*.

In that 1998 release, the capital L., still one third of the Fugees at the time, delivered the most unflinchingly personal, soul-exposing release of the era. In her case, she was spreading wisdom garnered from painful history. Thus the CD took its title from Carter G. Woodson's classic black history text *The Miseducation of the Negro*. While hip hop had de-volved into a showcase of scarred spirits, a flinch dealership, Lauryn moved way beyond that territory, opened up and showed herself as a casualty of love who has, nonetheless, learned some things. If there was a demon to be exorcized in the span of these sixteen tracks, it was the ghost of relationships past—a subject so radically at odds with the adolescent bullshit that is contemporary hip hop that *Miseducation* existed as hip hop at the same time as it challenged—or obliterated—the boundaries of the genre.

The most emotionally pointed sentiments came on songs where Lauryn opted to sing rather than utilize her gift for the verbals. At least five songs make reference to love betrayed by an unnamed "ex-factor," widely presumed to be fellow Fugee Wyclef Jean. But rather than settle for wrenching your soul for emotion and then evaporating, the artist sticks around, imbues her listener with the belief that she's healed herself and is stronger for the experience. Woven between her songs are outtakes of her fellow New Jerseyan Ras Baraka talking to elementary school students about the nature of love. Her willingness to love, her constant awareness of the imperative that black people dare to love, bears witness to the fact that at least one rapper has read James Baldwin and taken his words to heart.

Miseducation worked because it achieved an organic fusion of styles and musics that was light-years ahead of many of the awkward R&B-

rap combinations congesting the airwaves at the time. Most of her tracks were hard to classify musically and her vocals seem set upon heightening the ambiguity. Confident in her ability to get the job done vocally *and* verbally, L. wasn't above playing head-games, slipping between the two, tap dancing on the borders. On "Superstar," an editorial on the music industry, she sings with a rapper's sense of staggered enunciation. In oblique references to Lil' Kim and the Lox's minor hit "Money, Power & Respect," she informs that "you could get the money/you could get the power/but keep your eyes on the final hour." Lauryn came off as the Anti-Kim, a woman who places her faith in her own fertile mind rather than a set of surgically enhanced glands.

Where Lil' Kim's career was built on the shock value—and in popular music shock is *valuable*—of making genital reference in public, Lauryn spoke deeply of her decision to bear a child at a point when many warned it would be disastrous to her career. "To Zion," a guitar-laced lullaby to her son, is the most personal song on a thoroughly personal album, a song that writes itself into your memory. A release such as this might easily slip into maudlin moments or collapse under the weight of its own mush. But tricky though it might be, she managed to transmit sentiment without coming off as sentimental.

And Lauryn, for all her youth when she released *Miseducation*, found herself ranked among the most lyrically gifted of rappers, bar none. She simply worked harder and brought more metaphor and allusion to the table—the brown girl is quicker than the lazy dogs of the field. The L. could rhapsodize about loves lost and, in a moment's notice, wax apocalyptic on "Final Hour." In a dizzying sequence over a wispy harp and a four-note guitar that's as ominous as a cold sweat, she orates,

> *I'm about to change the focus*
> *from the richest to the brokest*
> *I wrote this opus to reverse the hypnosis.*

Where hip hop had all but devolved into a gauche player's ball, Lauryn Hill was trying to up the level of dialogue. Many are the biblical references and allusions to matters of the spirit.

On "Nothing Matters," she employed the neo-soul of D'Angelo for a sedate departure. It is a song on the blissful nonchalance of love that plays with the contrast between D'Angelo's ethereal vocals and high-end keys and Lauryn's denser vocal phrasings. You know D'Angelo is speaking of a love jones supreme when he says, "My team could score/make it to the final four/ repossess my 4x4/Nothing matters."

A funk-descended track supports "Every Ghetto, Every City," a cut that is given over to reminiscence of her childhood in New Jersey. Her vision here did for rap what Walter Mosley's *Always Outnumbered* did for fiction: provide a vision of black city people that is textured, complex, human. The people inhabiting her memories have flesh and blood. They smile. They hurt and dream. This is, perhaps, the sound of rap filtered through a young single mother's soul. Few are the male rappers willing to speak of the joy and vulnerability of parenthood; Lauryn speaks of being honored that a new life chose to navigate its way into the world via her womb. Like a handful of other artists that emerged in that era— Erykah Badu, Maxwell, D'Angelo—Lauryn Hill was intent upon moving urban music out of the kiddie pools and into deeper waters. *Miseducation* was way past the shallow end of things, and we would be blessed were more artists similarly *Miseducated.* This much we know.

But for that and a whole lot of other reasons, the sophomore effort, *MTV Unplugged 2.0,* was hard to listen to. Literally hard to listen to. The second release found the artist eschewing her former ways, dismissing her indelible style as simple vanities, and delivering her vocals with the accompaniment of only her own unmastered guitar. It was not coincidental that she began, at this point, to declare that she was no longer an "entertainer." For the observers up in the gallery, the guitar and the reggae-tinted vocals on *Unplugged* attested to the growing influence of Bob Marley on her music. Hill might've been channeling Marley, whose body of work had clearly influenced the entire Fugees collective, but there was more than that going on. Where non-believers criticized *Miseducation* for its preachiness, *Unplugged* was virtually a church revival. Her abiding concern with evildoers and the worldly wickedness that would surely not escape God's final judgment combined with her teary interludes made *Unplugged* an open wound of an album.

Soul music has consecutively nominated tormented male souls— Sam Cooke, Otis Redding, Marvin Gaye—to iconic status, but even within that field the image of a woman laying bare her spirit scars was unsettling. The romantic mythology even held that one could not sing soul music convincingly *unless* one had done some suffering, but no one ever dreamed of laying that kind of prereq on a rap artist.

Hip hop has its own life cycle of "blowing up" and "falling off," which equate to the rise and decline of one's artistic standing. After selling a reported fifteen million records with *The Score* and twelve million copies of *Miseducation, Unplugged,* which the less charitable referred to as *Undone,* was seen as a critical and commercial failure. In reality, though, *Unplugged* was not so much a case of falling off as it was melting down, with the artist literally breaking into tears midway through her performance and punctuating her songs with rambling sermons and biblical metaphors on the nature of life and suffering. Seeing Hill in live performance at that point in her career, it was hard to overlook that shadows of Hathaway and Holiday who were at least as much in attendance as Marley's spirit was.

However it was sliced, it was clear that there was no hip hop precedent for where she was going. She had already elasticized the understanding of what hip hop could be and helped return it to the R&B roots. As part of the Fugees, she had already insisted that hip hop be understood as a product of the Caribbean Diaspora. She had already established herself in the ranks of the most lyrically lacerating MCs. (Only the most gender-backward still applied the modifier "female" after the word "great" and before the word "MC" when speaking of her.)

The album was hailed more for its honesty than its artistic value. (Marvin Gaye could not have been more honest than he was on "Sanctified Lady" but that release was proof that great pain did not automatically produce great art.) The loose talk held that the bitter tone of the release was a product of marital strife and infidelity. But *Miseducation* was informed by a struggle with relationship discord as well. She may have drawn upon that drama to produce the brilliance of that release, but the subsequent one appeared to be overwhelmed by it. The cynical shook their heads and called it a case of Too Much Too Soon. Whatever the accuracy or inaccuracy of that kind of armchair diagnosis might be, the fact remained that even at that point, she was standing outside the conventional categories. With *Unplugged,* L was once again blazing trails. Whether those stony paths led to a place that her hip hop would willingly follow was another matter entirely.

JAY-Z: THE BLUEPRINT

For black men, beseeching America to recognize black humanity went out of style on April 4, 1968—which might explain why Shawn Carter, born December 4 the following year, has always been less interested in

seeking absolution than in having the charges against him thrown out al-
together. Or, to twist his own lyrical phrasing, to *justify his thug.* Such is
his pre-eminent concern that even as he states that there is no defense for
his crimes against the black community he is, of course, presenting one:

> *I can't justify genocide*
> *But I was born in a city where the skinny Niggas die.*

Then again, this is what you expect from an artist who titled his debut
release *Reasonable Doubt.*

Jay-Z's whole body of work—you might even say his artistic rationale—is concerned with the moral explication of the hustler's trade.
Marcy Projects loom over Bed-Stuy literally and metaphorically, visible
from the elevated J train tracks. Blue-Orange New York City Housing
Authority sign announcing that you've arrived in case you thought you
were still on the Upper West Side. The MC played himself up as a representative of it as much as the old-time ward bosses and machine
politicians were in their time, as if the projects had an at-large rep to the
rest of the world. Listen to the blistering "Where I'm From," the most
volatile street banger on his sophomore effort, *In My Lifetime, Vol. I,* and
you can't miss the argument that Marcy gave him probable cause for
whatever dirt he did before remaking himself as a rap artist.

Reasonable Doubt occupies the same niche as *Illmatic*—no matter the
amount of water under the bridge between the two artists that produced those classics. Both exist as brilliant artistic statements that prefaced the long slide into commercial considerations and an increasingly
ambivalent relationship to the standard definitions of hip hop *realness.*
But while *Illmatic* saw Nas, the young prodigy, delivering what had
been expected of him all along, by the time *Reasonable Doubt* reached
shelves, Jay-Z was already a journeyman in the field. The brilliance of
the release came like that of another fabled denizen of the Borough of
Kings, Sandy Koufax, who pitched for six undistinguished years in the
majors before finding his stride and becoming virtually unbeatable. To
be short with it, when *Reasonable Doubt* dropped, the rookies taking
their cuts at the game weren't quite sure what had blown past them. A
classic that no one saw coming.

Consider the fact that Jay is chronologically less than three years
younger than his mic mentor Big Daddy Kane, but artistically, Jay-Z's
era comes a millennium after that of Kane. Irrespective of his standing

as commercial icon, Jay-Z was familiar with the rough side of that mountain, spending years as an MC apprentice in the camps of Kane and later Jaz-O. KRS-One was content to announce the number of rhyme styles he had, but Jay took an evolutionary approach to rhyme. And as late as 1995, on the single "In My Lifetime," Jay-Z was showcasing a rhyme style that still bore Kane's aesthetic fingerprints, deliberately overstuffing his bars with too many syllables, dropping lyrics in swift, staccato-smooth displays. But by the time he began the recording sessions for *Reasonable Doubt* less than a year later, he was laying down something unique, putting together densely constructed lines with multiple meanings, but flowing like a deliberative old man who had all the time in the world to make his point. Inside those 365 days the staggered enunciation and the bars overstuffed with syllables evaporated, replaced by an approach so casual that it sounds more like a late-night radio DJ intro-ing a Chi-Lites selection. In a word, *Reasonable Doubt* saw Jay-Z present himself stylistically as the *anti*-Kane.

When the books are written, it will have to be acknowledged that Jay-Z was probably the most complete microphone artist of his generation of MCs—with the prior knowledge that in popular music, generations are measured in dog years. And, no, we're not measuring his standing on the basis of umpteen platinum records because if that was the criterion, Nelly, Will Smith, and Master P would find themselves in that same company, and his closest peers in terms of pure lyrical talent—your Commons, Kwelis, and Pharoahe Monchs—would be excluded by light years. No, this is about more than simply moving units off the music store shelves.

But the dilemma in dealing with Jay-Z as an artist is his status as a hustler. Even when encountering the MC at his most fragile—the confessions of wounded fatherlessness and his tormented moral meanderings about his days as a crack dealer—you confront the cynical question of whether this is live or Memorex. Or to cut to the substance of the issue, the question is whether this is the high water mark of his art or his vulnerability shtick. Spirit pain sells. Either way, it works—for the same reason that art has been working for eons: by raising more questions than it answers. Worse case scenario, this is a sales pitch from a cat selling you the Brooklyn Bridge—and if his game is polished enough, you'll make a down payment just for the hell of it.

In his various mic incarnations, he has hailed himself as the black Ralph Lauren, the black Warren Buffett, and, most recently, the black

JFK. If Jay-Z is the sepia version of the American baron, then that whole hustler question becomes a whole lot easier to resolve. Still, it's hard doubt the man as long as "You Must Love Me" or "Meet the Parents" is echoing in your brain. Then there is the jaded street ennui of "D'evils," a confessional on *Reasonable Doubt* that was matched by the self-evident "Regrets." That same theme was reprised on "A Week Ago," a song where he reprised the betrayal of an ally who turns snitch in the face of prison time.

But before you can sign off on an acquittal, consider the evidence of tracks like "Rap Game/Crack Game" on *In My Lifetime, Vol. I* and "U Don't Know" on *The Blueprint*, where he patiently explains that he can

> *Sell ice in the winter time, fire in hell*
> *I am a hustler baby, I'll sell water to a well.*

In certain quarters, where the questionable debates over "commercial" and "underground" get played out, Jay-Z was long ago consigned to the holding pen of "pop" rappers. Given his knack for crafting radio-friendly singles, the indictment is understandable. But if that label sticks, it has to also be said that he and Eminem were probably the first acts in hip hop's history to find equilibrium between their core audience and their mainstream one. That is to say, Jay-Z's work was deliberately, even ironically, pop, crossover with a wink and a nod. You can't get more confectionery than a Broadway show tune, but he did just that with the single "Hard Knock Life," jacking a snippet from *Annie* and forcing her to narrate his tale of Bed-Stuy privation. The artist proclaimed in an advertisement to have gotten his MBA from Marcy Projects. True indeed, there was a sophisticated market logic behind the product the artist put on the street. When critics held that the double-album *Blueprint²* was bloated and thick around the middle, Roc-A-Fella responded with *The Blueprint 2.1*, a tighter, trimmed-down single album that excised the least marketable material from the earlier version.

It was clear long before the public ascent of Jay-Z that the ethic, wits, and savvy of the street hustler were adaptable to other areas of endeavor, but it's equally apparent that the MC took that truth to a whole new level. That kind of smooth transitioning had the listener half expecting him to pen a self-help book called *The Hustler's Way*.

But to extend the hustle metaphor, *The Black Album*—his declared final release—was an attempt to make one last score before leaving the game. Tradition has it that the music industry be done with a talent before that talent is done with the industry. And in hip hop, where the average career lasts for fewer than two albums, the stakes are a quantum degree higher. Which returns us to the question of Jay-Z's enduring significance to the form. The hustler, like the chess player, is required to think two moves ahead of the current scenario. Even as his standing atop hip hop's pantheon was being solidified, the sands were shifting and the artist phrased his exit as the equivalent of retiring with the belt. For what it matters, *The Black Album* delivered most of what it promised, even as confections like "Change Clothes" and "Dirt Off Your Shoulder" interfere with what could have been the most brilliant hip hop offering in years. It was fitting, if unsatisfying, that his magnum opus be watered down by commercial considerations. Marciano famously retired while still an undefeated champion and decades of pugilists have tried in vain to imitate that example. No doubt, the MC was seeking that kind of permanence and his audience might be of a mind to grant it. But the jury is still out on that question.

BIG PUN: RETURN TO THE ESSENCE

Dateline: the Bronx. The land where hip hop began and Amadou Diallo was ended. 'Round these parts, Big Pun, the grand, obese, and deceased *Boriqua* wordsmith, is played like an ethnic hero in the tradition of DiMaggio and Al Smith. The big man checked out on February 7, 2000, apparently victimized by his reported 792 pounds just a few scant weeks before the release of his sophomore CD. And everywhere in the borough, from the head shops in White Plains and the *caridad* restaurants on Fordham to the beeper joint on Gun Hill and the shotgun bodegas down on Third Avenue, the question was the same: *You heard Pun is dead, yo?*

The Punisher's star was in mid-ascent elsewhere in the world, but in the home field of the boogie down (aka the Bronx) the man had already achieved boulevard demigod status, putting in appearances at the Puerto Rican Day Parade and getting hailed like a foreign dignitary. Ripping up shows at the Apollo, leaving the crowd chanting his cross-ethnic catchphrase: *Boriqua, Morena, Boriqua, Morena* . . . Puerto Rican, black—a reminder to all of hip hop's Latino lineage.

Arriving in the late 90s, at a point when KRS-One was the sole representative of hip hop's native soul who still had a national audience,

Capital Punishment, the big man's debut, established him as an artist to be contended with. Like a small number of his peers, he was able to supply commercial vehicles like "I'm Not A Player," a collaboration with the R&B artist Joe, as well as certified street anthems. Pun's rhyme lineage connected him to the under-appreciated DITC, or Diggin In The Crates crew, a squad of aesthetic throwbacks who brought to the fore the old styles that hip hop had been founded upon, with minor adaptations to the new era. Repping the Bronx and uptown Manhattan, like the rightful heirs to Melle Mel, Spoonie G., and Busy Bee, the DITC artists—Fat Joe, Lord Finesse, Showbiz & AG, Diamond D and Big L.— were defined by their existence just below the commercial radar.

Pun, on the other hand, had been put on by his fellow Latin artist Fat Joe and become an immediate commercial force. Here was a rapper cut from yards of the old fabric, a throwback to the era when MCs were battle-tested in the crucible of illegal schoolyard jams, when one's rep was established by inflicting verbal humiliation on all comers, not by faxing a bold-printed press release. Fact is that Big Pun and his Terror Squad brethren represented the best shot the Bronx had at recapturing a trace of its bygone glory as the birthplace of hip hop. And the untimely departure of the big-boned bard leaves the Squad minus its clean-up hitter, and the borough minus its street statesman.

Take a minute to listen to *Yeeeah Baby,* presumably his final opus and what comes across is how deeply schooled in the art of verbal ass-kicking the big man was, issuing threats to "run up in your crib with the gun out/spray up your peeps/and smack the baby teeth out your son's mouth." The subject matter is the same blend of ribald scenario and offer-you-can't-refuse overtures to the blistered hip hop wannabes that he brought to the table on *Capital Punishment,* but this release is edgier. *Yeeeah Baby* features only two of the mellowed out R&B-seasoned cuts that Pun rode to platinum glory on *Capital Punishment.* On the keyboard-driven "It's So Hard" Pun divides the labor with LaFace Records crooner Donnell Jones and turns in a track destined for heavy rotation among his avenue constituents.

But *Yeeeah Baby* was a project bequeathed to the brethren. Having won over the women with his ear-friendly debut, the Punisher came back with a lil' something for the brothers. And came off with it. Check out Pun, staying on top of the tracks, buzzing through hyper-kinetic rhyme flows and never chasing his breath despite his Sumo-sized physique. Next the big man is claiming to have songs written by the devil with Jesus singing the chorus. The beats turned in by an ad-hoc committee of producers are an aural collage of bells, whistles, chimes, and heavy-metal guitar, and unlike most multi-produced projects, the sounds on this one come together like pieces of a musical jigsaw puzzle. That said, it's unspeakably eerie to hear the boasts of a dead man bellowing from a set of speakers, especially the ironic moment at the end of "It's So Hard" when Pun brags, "I just lost a hundred pounds and I ain't goin' nowhere. I wanna live."

Big Pun did in fact live, with the proceeds of his debut turning him into a ghetto extravagant and thickening his mid-section. And it is this life of asphalt grandeur and jealous suckers that provides the theme for *Yeeeah Baby*. Early on, he warns that he's "400 pounds, but I move fast" and proceeds to tear through the heavy metal–laced intro song "Watch Those" with enough agility of tongue to leave an auctioneer envious. Truth told, the entire CD is defined by an uncommon density of rhyme; *Yeeah Baby* is a catalog of internal rhymes and swift double entendres. In one typically staggered, rapid-fire riff, Pun vows to leave his rivals "dead before the body falls/cause when the shottie roars/I ignore/Giuliani's laws." On the thick, menacing, and eminently jeepable "We Don't Care," Pun trades verses with fellow Terror Squad initiate Cuban Link and the duo put on an ebonic poetry clinic. Backed by a hint of Spanish guitar, Pun pledges to "word to a junkie's mama/I'ma keep it funky for his homies [doing time] in Elmira." His partner in rhyme spins tales of the poor and unlawful, charging, "I'm nothin' but a hustler/burning rubber with drugs stuffed up the muffler/shut the fuck up/or get a slug in the jugular."

Excepting the mindless juvenilia of songs like "My D**K," Pun managed to successfully tap dance on that thin line between a commercially doomed underground classic and commercially driven ghetto hyperbole. On "Leather Face," he returns to the heavy metal–tinged sound of "Watch Those," but adds a whistling keyboard backdrop and percussive piano hits for a sinister, horror-flick feel. A step later, Pun floats his verbals on the light, Salsa spiced "100%"—a bilingual cut turned in just in case you doubted his ability to flip it *en español*.

The tragedy underlying the absolute fatness of the man's body of work is that the artist swerved around the pothole known as the sophomore jinx, only to end up as the latest late rapper of the season. In hip hop, premature death has become a cliché. Another aerosol epitaph.

Another visage thrown up on the barren walls near Westchester Avenue—right next to Biggie and Tupac.

COMMON: THE ART OF RESURRECTION

A great artist doesn't always provide you with art that you like, but always with art that are you interested in talking about. Over the course of his first six releases, Common, the pioneering MC hailing from the Windy City, struggled to produce work that could be declared equal to his great talent. The results were uneven, brilliant at points, far from the mark at others, but almost always worthy of discussion. Between his 1992 debut *Can I Borrow A Dollar?* and *Resurrection*, released two years later, Common Sense (who would soon drop the "sense" from his title) arguably evolved more than any major artist in the genre had in a similar span. More than any of his peers, his body of work yields a clear artistic progression from one LP to the next, like flipping through the family album and watching an adolescent mature into manhood.

The Common of *Can I Borrow A Dollar?* was intoxicated with his own verbal inventiveness. Case and point: the remix for "Soul by the Pound" reveals the artist heavily under the influence of the Brooklyn duo Das Efx, delivering multiple puns and entendres per verse: "I got skills like Tim and I'm coming in the hard-a-way/so keep the crossover." His skill for triple-layered references came off as more showy and adolescent than those delivered by deep thinkers like Rakim or Nas. His streaming line of slick references and veiled allusions played big with hip hop's literary criticism crowd, but the album literally was not *about* anything. It featured the standard arrangements of braggardry ("Charms Alarm") and bitch-vilification ("Heidi Hoe"). And if you missed the point, he graces the back jacket of the CD posed with the requisite forty-ounce malt liquor bottle sheathed in a paper bag. Despite those simplicities, the release leaves the frustrating suspicion that, unlike his peers, Common Sense was actually capable of thinking deeper than that. It was as if he found himself lyrically dressed to the nines with nowhere to go; the young MC contented himself by sitting on the stoop, brave talking and boasting with the boys in the hood. Advance word held that the Chicagoan was the MC who would finally put the second city on that hip hop map. But his debut could be considered groundbreaking for that—and only that—reason.

In fairness, early Common was representative of a hip hop–wide adolescent streak that preferred to consign women to the category of simple sex objects rather than grapple with female complexity (and risk getting joked on by one's boys). That explains why Common wasted an aphrodisiac riff from the Isley Brothers' "Between the Sheets" on the juvenile "Breaker 1/9"—a sample that Biggie later put to good, woman-charming use on "Juicy."

It was impossibly ironic that Common's future rep would be as a "backpack" rapper, a semi-underground artist who catered more to the tofu and patchouli crowd than to the brew-swilling brothers holding it down in the Cabrini Greens of the world. But *Resurrection* was the first step in that progression. His earlier incarnation brought to mind that other laureled Chicagoan, Michael Jordan, who early on was content to display his virtuoso balling ability and dunk on nearly every possession, even in the midst of a losing effort. The Common of *Resurrection* understood that there was more to the game than simply offense.

The cliché tells that "less is more," but in taming his urge toward cleverness, he delivered greater overall impact. "Watermelon," the second track on the release, was a verbal victory lap that threw down the lyrical gauntlet far more effectively than anything he offered on *Can I Borrow A Dollar?* Speaking of his talent for delivering rhymes with layers of significance that dawned on you way down the line, he said, "My style is similar to AIDS/You eff with it now, but catch it later." The evidence of his quantum leap in development was seen not just in his increased mastery of his form, but in his content as well. With something to actually talk about, he came off as more reflective, an artist tenuously venturing off the block into the broader world.

Resurrection featured Common's first bona fide love song, though the object of his affections is an *it* not a *she*. Devoted to his love of the hip hop itself, the deftly metaphorical "I Used To Love H.E.R." delivered his first legitimate hit song and an audience broader than the male lyric-decoding cognoscenti who bought his first album. With *Resurrection*, you still heard the ambivalence toward emotional commitment ("I spend great time with the rhyme/More than any female") but you also hear apologias like "I had to halt with the/Malt liquor" and the declaration that he had "un-swined" his diet.

It was interesting to note that a love song on *Resurrection*, not any of the gonad-grabbing drive-bys he'd performed on *Can I Borrow A Dollar?*, generated his first conflict with another established artist. Taking exception to the way Common had phrased hip hop's migration to the West Coast on "I Used To Love H.E.R.," Ice Cube made the mistake of issuing "Slaughterhouse," a dis record aimed at the Chicago native. Common's response was swift, brutal, and as unsparing as the takedown of Sonny Corleone in *The Godfather*. With "I See the Bitch in You," he took full control of his skill for lyrical assault, creating one of the all-time hip hop classic battle records. Evidence of his evolving political temperament and the broad palette he was drawing his material from was seen in "A Song for Assata," a tribute to the black revolutionary who was shot, incarcerated, and daringly escaped to freedom in Cuba.

Resurrection was the release in which he most evenly balanced the perspective of a thoughtful young poet with that of an MC, deeply schooled in hip hop's tradition of verbal manslaughter. That tension is decreasingly present in his subsequent *One Day It'll All Make Sense* and *Like Water For Chocolate*, the release that most firmly entrenched him in the ranks of hip hop's "progressive" underground. Whether that adjective was fitting (or if it even existed) was debatable, but by the late 90s Common's name was consistently mentioned in tandem with similarly tagged artists Black Thought, Talib Kweli, Mos Def, and Pharoahe Monch. Either way, "progressive" was not the adjective that was attached to his subsequent release, *Electric Circus*.

Deliberately abstract and conceptually broad as Lake Michigan, *Electric Circus* was an attempt to widen the boundaries of what constituted hip hop. Produced in the main by ?uestlove of the Roots, the CD aspired to be hip hop's equivalent of *Purple Rain* or *Are You Experienced?* In the context of the Roots' efforts on *Phrenology*, Mos Def's *Black on Both Sides*, which featured heavy rock riffs and frantic guitar interludes, Q-Tip's never-released *Kamaal the Abstract*, and the genre-bending efforts of neo-soulsters like Jill Scott and Common's then-partner Erykah Badu, there was every reason to believe that hip hop was ready for that kind of expansion. That might have been the case, but it was equally true that with *Electric Circus* Common's reach exceeded his grasp. *EC* was flawed in an ironic way, guilty of precisely the opposite offenses than those committed on *Can I Borrow A Dollar?* The latter was so grounded that it was myopic. The former was so ethereal that it was difficult to hold onto. Listening to the two releases in tandem would sound like the artist had abandoned the South Side of Chicago and moved to the suburbs of Jupiter.

But the most damning commentary about *Circus* was simultaneously its greatest praise. He could have played it safe and produced eleven more tracks designed for hood heavy-rotation and been praised as a lyrical man among boys. Instead, he opted to steer into the headwinds of hip hop's homophobia with songs like "Between Me, You & Liberation." The howling damnation of that effort left even Common himself stating that he had gone too far out conceptually. The color commentary declared that he had been unduly influenced by Badu, but truth told, tracks from *Like Water For Chocolate* like "Nag Champa" and "Time Travelin," an homage to Fela Kuti, hinted at Common's artistic trajectory long before *EC*. And even if his reach exceeded his grasp, the fact remained that he was at least reaching, and in the hip hop of the early millennium, expansion was far from a given.

By the time he delivered *Be*, his sixth release, the weight of representing the Windy City was at least partially taken from his shoulders. Artists like Twista, the R&B stylist R. Kelly, and especially Kanye West had crafted a more democratic musical order. Produced almost entirely by West, *Be* marked a return to form, even if it was a safe effort by hip hop standards. In artistic terms, *Be* was almost a second *Resurrection*. But the Common of "Watermelon" and "I See the Bitch in You" made only cameo appearances on *Be*. In his place he delivered a series of commentaries on the state of his hood and his people, a series of human images that were only seen in the hip hop's better moments. If he's less interested in lacerating lesser MCs it's because he has more weighty concerns on his mind. From the vantage point of *Be*, the early work looks small in the same way that your third-grade classroom does when you see it a dozen years later. Whether the release constituted the artistic greatness that had been awaited since his arrival thirteen years earlier was still subject to discussion. And on some level, that was already evidence enough.

EMINEM: RACE MAN

In the pantheon of disposable American heroes, Marshall Mathers is the man of the moment. Having turned a media double play on the big screen and the airwaves with the high-grossing biopic *8 Mile* and its ubiquitous soundtrack, M.M. (or Eminem) parlayed his anointed fifteen minutes into an epic run of at least several hours. Having been canonized in the pages of the *New York Times* and virtually ordained by the glossies, digging Eminem became hipness litmus. Frank Rich, in the midst of a pathos festival in the pages of the *Times*, praised Em's lyrical flow and originality. En route to proclaiming Eminem as fun for all ages, he offered this observation:

> In a country in which broken homes, absentee parents and latchkey kids are endemic to every social class, he can touch some of the hottest emotional buttons. He can be puerile too, but what else is new in pop music?

No less an authority on hip hop than Andrew Sullivan observed on Salon.com that

> Eminem's music is some of the most challenging, inventive and lyrically brilliant in recent times. His movie . . . was an excellently written and directed product. There's no mystery why it did so well.

With the minor concerns of his anti-gay and violently misogynistic lyrics airbrushed into obscurity courtesy of endorsements by critics, Em's slouchy way and disaffected scowl were set to become the modern equivalent of Elvis's hip tic.

Dig, way back before the Beastie Boys had ever heard of Tibet, they were the hip hop equivalent of a minstrel show, pimping black style in absurdly hyperbolic character acting. Vanilla Ice was long ago consigned to the trashbin of blackface mockery. Lest there be any question where Eminem stands among the blackfacers, he writes, "I'm fed up, lately I'm on edge/I grabbed Vanilla Ice and ripped out his blond dreads."

No question, his debut, *The Slim Shady LP,* was a blistering, brilliantly ignorant, sublime, backward, funk-laden, and retrograde example of a young man having dialogue with his demons. Eminem came off as a sort of spiritual cousin of the late Notorious One, albeit a cousin from a side of the family the obese man never knew about. *The Slim Shady LP* will bring to mind the part in Albert King's "Born Under a Bad Sign" when the bluesman wails that

> *I been down ever since the day I could crawl*
> *and if it wasn't for bad luck*
> *I probably wouldn't have no luck at all.*

With *Slim Shady* Eminem either put together a deeply honest rendition of the white trash blues or pulled off the slickest, most minstrelized con job conceivable.

And like his portly counterpart, the content of Eminem's material is way beyond troubling. The release alternated between profound commentary and complete stupidity, between misogyny and the personal despair that will inevitably be cited as the source of it. The rapper is disillusioned, gleefully underdeveloped and terminally maladjusted with a gift for expressing these facts creatively. Case in point, on "If I Had" the kid gives voice to the bleakness of urban existence in the late twentieth century, stating, "I'm tired of being white trash/broke and always poor/I'm tired of having to take bottles back to the store."

One track later he is idiotically fantasizing about kidnapping his daughter, murdering his baby-mother, and creating a series of lies to explain to the child why her mother has had her throat slit and been dumped in the ocean. In a genre that prides itself upon absurdist fantasy, this is without a doubt the most perverse and twisted exploration I've ever heard—a fact that he will, no doubt, take as a compliment. The CD cover, in fact, features a picture of the rapper and his little girl standing on a pier, presumably preparing to dump momma, whose dead foot juts from the car trunk. While artists routinely jump the starter's pistol in a race to the bottom, Eminem's gender politics dwell in a sub-basement. This is a man who refers to his own mother as a cunt. Recognizing the potential for controversy as a sales tactic, it hard to believe that the flick wasn't contrived to offend—which nonetheless does nothing to reduce the fact that Eminem looks damn near fetal in his underdevelopment.

The problem, as always, came when he was declared to be a genius. Hailed as such in the pages of *Rolling Stone,* his homophobic ranting became so inconsequential that he could be canonized by Sullivan—a gay white Republican who first published Murray and Herrnstein's *The Bell Curve* in the pages of *The New Republic.*

Conventional journalism about Eminem held that each second paragraph be reserved for statements about his disturbing significance to our particular cultural moment and the important questions his ascent raises. Long pause. Truth told, beyond asking the obvious questions (i.e., Yo, they, like, got white people in Detroit?) the response from black hip hop cognoscenti was an audible yawn. True, the rapper's cultural cache has earned him placement on the covers of underground hip hop publications, but their treatment of him has had way fewer hosannas than the mainstream magazines and papers that have branded him as the second coming of Elvis Marciano.

Compare Rich and Sullivan's assessment to this unsolicited testimonial from a black writer on the Afrofuturism listserv:

> I know that we are on the list to talk about futurist themes in Black cultural production. And right now with all this Eminem talk I think the eradication of white hegemony would be quite futuristic. Does anyone have any links to any articles where the writer has actually told the truth about this %$#@!())&???

Mainstream American pop has been dipping into black culture for reinvigoration since the days of burnt cork; that a white rapper has made millions is nothing new.

Eminem's market dominance occurred for the same reasons that Jayson "White Chocolate" Williams of the Sacramento Kings had the best selling jersey in the NBA that year, and I'm awaiting the day that music critics start praising Eminem for having "sound fundamentals" when it comes to rapping. Both Em and Williams were the beneficiaries of a type of cultural affirmative action for white men, which is to say that neither of them was unqualified, but both are object lessons in the benefits of diversity. (Toddlers too small to grip a microphone or hold a basketball now will in future days remember the first time they heard Eminem flow or saw one of Williams' pyrotechnic, no-look passes and realized that they too could succeed in a black-dominated world.)

Eminem is neither the first commercially successful white rapper—the Beastie Boys lay claim to that distinction—nor the first charged with the Elvising of hip hop (that would be Vanilla Ice). He fits into a pantheon of white artists that include moderate successes like Third Base (a riff on the famous "Who's on First?" routine) and the Irish American trio House of Pain, who played up their Gaelic ancestry as an ethnic counterpoint to the Afrocentrism that dominated hip hop at the time. But the question remains: who *is* on first? Eminem is in scoring position because he is, for what it matters, probably the most talented white rapper to yet emerge. But comparing Eminem to the lineage of white wordsmiths is approximately as patronizing as calling Miles Davis a fine Negro musician or referring to Denzel Washington as that black guy with the Oscar.

Eminem is undoubtedly clever, but cleverness is as common to rappers as lying is to politicians. His flow is infectious, but not in the same league as vocal masters like Rakim. Em has a lyrical gift, but leave him in the same room with Common or Talib Kweli and you'd have a repeat of the Larry Holmes-Gerry Cooney fight back in '82. Nor does Eminem himself have any illusions about his standing in the pantheon of rap, having stated in interviews that he doesn't consider himself to be in the top tier of rappers in terms of skill.

What Em sold—and what has resonated with his legions of fans, salivating critics, and assorted media apostles—is a narrative of worthless childhood in the post-industrial wasteland of the former Motor City. With his brooding, swaggering persona, replete with prereq tattoos, oversized gear, and bleached-out follicles, Eminem has been appointed the voice of Anglo angst a la Kurt Cobain—Columbine chic.

In a country where class distinctions are consistently glossed over and the white poor are virtually invisible, save for the sardonic exploitation of Jerry Springer, Eminem's trailer park blues have way more significance to white suburban America than hip hop as a genre. For what it matters, Eminem's tales of alienation (i.e., his existential query "How can I be white when I don't even exist?") descend from the visceral autobiographical narratives of rappers like Scarface, Notorious B.I.G., and Tupac Shakur. At its best, hip hop has been a vehicle for expressing—and transcending—the frailties and the pain of life in the negative space of America. But that reality was lost on many prior to the Eminem movement. To be accurate, Eminem may fit into that tradition of lyrical catharsis and boulevard jeremiads, but he damn sure ain't create it. Plus, Em's matricidal ramblings are beyond the pale even for hip hop; gangsta rappers, like their celluloid counterparts, will consistently take hiatus from issuing colorful death threats to pay homage to dear old mom. (See Tupac's "Dear Mama" or Biggie's loving nod to his mother on "Juicy.")

Epidermal novelty explains why mainstream critics, baby boomers, and other people who are not in hip hop's core demographic are purchasing Eminem records. To cut to the quick: white pain became the flavor of the month and if oppression (class, that is, not race, sexual orientation, or gender) leaves a man with some rough misogynist and homophobic edges, what can you expect? He's *poor* for God's sake. Sympathy for the black poor (and the stories they tell) may have gone out with bell bottoms and eight track tapes but a *white* poor guy raises questions that are both unsettling and alluring to Market America (i.e., Didn't FDR take care of that problem?) One can imagine Rich and Sullivan sipping Merlot in their respective dens while grooving to the *8 Mile* soundtrack and asking, "Yo, they, like, still got white people in Detroit?"

The digital mytho-history of *8 Mile* played up this class angle—with substantial echoes of Prince's cult classic *Purple Rain*. Trailer park denizen Jimmy Smith—a stand-in for our lyrical hero—inhabits a perpetually overcast world where opportunity lost its lease. Down but not completely out, B. Rabbit—Jimmy's performance alter ego—struggles nobly to be judged by the content of his lyrics, not the color of his skin. Jimmy has no racial reckoning of his own to do because racism is black people's problem in *8 Mile*. Jimmy loves everybody. He even takes up for a gay guy at work. The climactic scene in which B. Rabbit outs his black male rival as a middle-class brat with a thug complex reminded me of that scene in *Rocky II* where another of America's low-income icons beats the ten-count to take the title from that rich flamboyant black guy. When you get right down to it, how bad can black people with money have it? With his gift for crossover appeal (though he's crossing class, not race lines), it's fitting that Eminem hails from Detroit—the city where Berry Gordy first came up with his formula for selling black music to white America.

The boy made a name for himself by suggesting he was chocolate on the inside, but he made a fortune from an audience invested in seeing him as white to the bone. Marshall Mathers: credit to his race.

THE NOTORIOUS ONE: STAY BLACK AND DIE

The arch bluesman Robert Johnson died at age twenty-seven under mysterious circumstances widely believed to have been foretold in his music. Christopher Wallace, known professionally as Notorious B.I.G., left this earth at twenty-four. His first album was titled *Ready to Die*. Big came up in Brooklyn, Bedford-Stuyvesant to be precise, a hard asphalt province whose citizens proudly call it "Do or Die Bed-Stuy." Biggie was fated, in short order, to fall into both those categories. The big man was a product of that hood, the oldest black community in New York City, founded by ex-slaves. Generations of negrophilic blues liberals have been enchanted by the devil lore of Robert Johnson, that the man brokered away his soul to old Beelzebub himself in exchange for musical mastery. Whatever else Biggie sold at the crossroads of Nostrand Avenue and Fulton Street, it wasn't his soul to the devil—at least not literally. His music told of the Faustian crack hustle he put down on Brooklyn streets corners—urban crossroads. But it was the willingness to grapple with the minus-zero reality of that world and the undiminished pain inherited by black dwellers of those nameless streets that set B.I.G. apart from his lyrically anemic peers.

In Brooklyn, death angels came draped in oversized Tommy Hil and Timberlands. There are ten thousand midnight troopers selling gethigh in the Borough of Kings, home to two million of New York's stories. Take a look at the infamous zones: Bed-Stuy, East New York, Red Hook, Flatbush, and Brownsville and it is obvious who owns the night. The burly Brooklynite professionally known as the Notorious B.I.G. was once one of those ranks. Way before the buppies and gentrification, before Spike Lee opened his "joint" and people with designer dreads moved next door, Fort Greene was the refuge of the buckwild with streets as dangerous as a shared needle. It was the city within a city where Big did his dirt and collected his cash. And it was those same streets that would brim with brown people lured out to witness the funeral procession of Christopher Wallace, aka Notorious B.I.G.

With a handful of exceptions, like the Houston-based Scarface and Tupac Shakur, the life of the black city dweller had not been expressed with artistic honesty in hip hop at that point. Think of the blistered second-person narration of Grand Master Flash and the Furious Five's "The Message" or Public Enemy's "Night of the Living Baseheads," and it becomes clear that by the early 90s hip hop's narration of the city had gone Hollywood. In the case of the late Notorious one, rarely before had an MC been honest enough to speak of the hellhounds on his trail, dogs fierce enough to leave a brother contemplating taking himself to an early grave. That fact essentially made him a blues rapper.

His now-classic *Ready to Die* opens with the sounds of a woman in labor, the subcurrent of Curtis Mayfield's *Superfly,* and the cries of a newborn. It closes with the gruesome report of a .38, the sickening thud of a body hitting the floor, perishing by its own hand. We hear the heartbeats slow and stop. The listeners shift uncomfortably as audio witness to a suicide. Even set against the shock-value interludes crammed onto nearly every hip hop CD, the final moments of *Ready to Die* are among the most disturbing in hip hop.

Between those two poles, birth and self-inflicted death, were seventeen tracks that etched out Big's history and worldview. The addition of B.I.G., along with Nas, Wu-Tang, and the Fugees, to the roster of New York MCs shored up the East Coast's fortunes at a time when L.A. and Oakland had all but become the dominant voices in the music industry. What set *Ready to Die* apart from the dozens of blathering, would-be playa releases was the combination of B.I.G.'s verbal virtuosity and his willingness to ascribe a level of vulnerability to himself that was, at that point, unparalleled.

Case and point: while NWA founder Eazy E was nagged by the ominously persistent cough and withering into nothingness, he was steadily spinning out yarns in which he played the immortal, almighty nigga supreme—Right up 'til that moment when HIV claimed his life. Minus exceptions like Ice Cube's morose "Dead Homiez," the pre-Notorious gangsta used hip hop as urban folklore in which he could write his name in the sky, render himself invincible, and stand out from the anonymous precincts of the ghetto. But only in the rarest of moments could hip hop give light to the fact that suicide trails only murder as a leading cause of death among black men between eighteen and twenty-five.

B.I.G. broke ranks with that. He spoke of pain anesthetized by malt liquor swilled to excess. *Ready to Die* was crass and backward, but it was also the forum for a sublime rapper to exorcise his demons, to lay bare his lacerated soul. He pushed lines like:

> *All my life I been considered as the worse*
> *lying to my mother, even stealing out her purse*
> *every crime known, from drugs to extortion*
> *I know my mother wish she had a fucking abortion.*

The rapper broods for three or four more verses then abruptly squeezes the trigger, canceling his own life.

Life After Death, his sophomore release, picks up—literally—where *Ready to Die* ends. We hear the emergency room drama and the rapper's final moments in an eerie prelude to what actually went down at an L.A. hospital in March 1997. Biggie appears on the CD cover, sporting a fedora and overcoat Hitchcock style, standing in front of a hearse. The twenty-four track double-disc release showcases Big's ability to rip rhymes from every conceivable angle, but the flashes of insight that redeemed its precursor are all but gone. *Life* would have easily have continued Big's ascent through the ranks of hip hop with its bicoastal flavor and mix of base-driven heaviness and melodic, R&B-suffused tracks. Almost as if to prove a point, Big shows up on "Mo Money Mo Problems" in Bone Thugs mode and proceeds to flip their style better than its originators. The irony of *Life* is Big's attempt to build a detente between the coasts musically and the fact that, at least indirectly, he became a casualty of that conflict. *Ready to Die* ended with Big's on-air suicide, *Life After Death* closes with a death threat being issued to Big and the rapper divining that "you're nobody 'til somebody kills you." In hip hop, martyrdom is the new black.

In real life, B.I.G. went out in a hail of bullets, none from his own gun. But that haunted reckoning with the reaper was all but predicted in the Big man's life and art. Filter through the weed smoke and hyperbole that swirls around hip hop and you recognize that death permeates these corners. Frail or not, all men are allergic to lead. And from this reality arises the attempt to immortalize oneself in song and story, to ensure that the tale of one's exploits will pass through the mouths of the generations of hustlers yet unborn. In hip hop, we find the rapper acting as his own griot and eulogist and running down his pedigree in the tradition of the old blues masters.

A vain hope that street legends will preserve one's name like amber to ancient mosquitoes.

Conclusion

One summer day in 2003, I stood in a slave castle and thought about Wu-Tang Clan. I was on Goree Island, in Senegal, West Africa, inside the stone holding pens where untold numbers of black human beings were stored before embarking upon the Middle Passage. The portal leading from the castle to the beach is called the "door of no return," the last vision of home that those men, women, and children would ever witness. Before them lay the yawning blue void of the Atlantic. Wandering on the island that afternoon I had come across a home that was being repaired: into the wet cement of the construction, children had scrawled a giant, elliptical "W." I recognized that symbol, but dismissed it as mere coincidence until I saw the words next to it: "Brooklyn Zoo." The "W" is the symbol for the nine-man ensemble called Wu-Tang Clan, the reference was to a single released by the late Russell Jones, aka Ol' Dirty Bastard. As I stood in the castle, I realized that not all returns are physical.

At its core, hip hop is a music of the African Diaspora, anchored in the musical principles preserved by that human cargo departing from Goree and passed down through ancestral generations. We could see that scrawled "W" as more evidence of globalism's viral spread throughout the far corners of our world. But I choose to see it in the same light that Tupac Shakur saw the rose that grew from concrete. I choose to see it as evidence of what Ahmed Sekou Touré called the "return to the source." Metaphorical, maybe, digital definitely, but a return nonetheless.

Thus, this is a book for all of us who have ever been hypnotized by a breakbeat, nodded our heads in a common choreography, gotten open to an MC with an absolutely ridiculous flow, had hip hop explain the world to us and us to it and then lamented where the art disappeared to. This book was written for all those who watched in frustration as the art offered itself up on the altar of economic expediency. In 2006, Prince

Paul, the visionary producer behind Stetsasonic, De La Soul, and the Handsome Boy Modeling School, eulogized the music, writing that "I really feel that the hip hop we love is dead." Hip hop has been declared to be dying almost since it was born, but hearing those bleak words from one with Prince Paul's standing is almost enough to make one break out the Bible, the black suit, and the hard-soled shoes. But what else could be the prognosis when you witness hip hop marginalia like Three 6 Mafia misogynize their way onto the Grand Stage and walk off with an Academy Award for predigested sop like "It's Hard Out Here For a Pimp"? What other conclusion can one draw when confronted by the neo-minstrelsy of a Lil' Jon and the profit-driven misanthropy of a 50 Cent and the near obscurity of brilliant artists like Jean Grae or Immortal Technique?

It is at these times that we have to remind ourselves of the creative urge that lies at the heart of hip hop. In her classic study *The Music of Black Americans*, Eileen Southern said of the black musical tradition:

> Again and again black musical styles have passed over into American music; there to be diluted and altered in ways that appeal to a wider public . . . The black composer's response has simply been to invent new music . . . the old is never totally discarded, however, but absorbed into the new.

Thus, the situation that hip hop faces is not new. In the worst-case scenario hip hop may drop into the vast well of commercial mediocrity but it will still inform the musical innovations that are surely to come. And as an idealist I choose to believe that our worst-case scenarios are not pre-ordained. Hip hop's struggle to maintain a fragment of its essence is the struggle we all confront in the first days of the twenty-first century. The music may well just be a sad microcosm of the off-kilter, market-saturated world we've created for ourselves. And instead of blaming we should instead hold ourselves accountable for allowing things to get to this bitter place.

In 1963, when LeRoi Jones published his landmark book *Blues People*, he could look back and appreciate the music in a way that escaped so many observers years earlier. This is the benefit of history. It is my hope that historians of some distant, future America will look back at hip hop and be amazed. The bullshit quibbling over its status as art will long ago have been settled. They'll easily understand the blues as the cornerstone upon which hip hop was erected, see clearly the jazz tradition of improvisation that informed the microphone arts of the MC. It will have become cliché to observe the blues and noir roots of hip hop's storytelling impulse and the exuberant funk spirit that breathed life into the form. They will easily connect the historical dots that dawned on this historian while standing in the slave castles of Goree Island decades earlier. That future historian will observe casually that in its most pure, pained, and truthful moments, you could divine the presence of the genius ancestors informing hip hop's self-expression.

What will still remain amazing is the spotlight hip hop shone on otherwise invisible lives. They will see hip hop as a primary source on the struggles, the losses, the joys, the frustrations, the glory, the vanity, the brilliance, vanity, beauty, and complex ugliness of life in the late twentieth century. That bright historian will write of the era in the early twenty-first century when many of its most devout listeners doubted its future. Those predictions proved inaccurate, she will point out, because of the revolutionary developments that took place in 2010. A footnote will inform the lay reader that it was in that year that an illegal park jam in the Bronx was organized by the son of slain DJ Scott La Rock and the daughter of the late Notorious B.I.G. A gray-haired man in his early fifties recalled a treasured bit of knowledge from his youth and jacked enough electricity from a nearby streetlight to power the amps, 808 speakers, and an antique set of Technique 1200 turntables. This jam led to the first International Freestyle Congress two years later in which a global array of MCs gathered in New York City for the equivalent of the MC Olympics. It was not until the delegations from Cuba and Brazil had silenced the heavily-favored Americans that the truth of hip hop's sad decline in the United States began to sink in. In 2011, the first hip hop cooperative was established in Las Vegas on the fifteenth anniversary of Tupac Shakur's death. The organization began with the goal of "eliminating commercial domination of our chosen art form and providing artists with an empowering outlet for their creative brilliance." The cooperatives split their profits equally with the artists and demanded that they adhere to a single guiding principle: "Above all else, tell the truth. Creatively." The 2016 Congress, held in Salvador de Bahia, Brazil, saw the Americans take silver. Gone were the days of their unquestioned microphone supremacy, but you had to admit that the tri-lingual kid from Chicago who flipped it in English, Spanish, and Portuguese put the United States back on the map.

Those years witnessed what scholars of the music came to call the Second Golden Age of Hip Hop. And as a final note, the historian will undoubtedly point out that those who doubted the music's future had their reasons, but they had also forgotten that this is a music created by survivors, people who had willed themselves in from the margins of America. Listen closely to hip hop and you could still hear rattling chains and the subversion of those who had first insisted upon creating beauty in a hostile land. Time would reassure them that their music was permanent. And it would remind them that when the first MCs had defiantly gripped the mic, shouting to the crowds "it don't stop, it won't stop" they were telling the absolute truth.

Shout Outs

This project grew out late night conversations with my colleagues Ayoka Chenzira and Beverly Guy-Sheftall on Goree Island that summer. I'm thankful to them for our meandering and contentious discussions of "their" music and "my" music (with the implicit understanding that it was really all *our* music). I am also thankful to the UNCF-Mellon Faculty Seminars for funding my participation in the seminar, on Pan-Africanist Aesthetics. Particular thanks go to Rudolph Byrd, Cynthia Spence, Tracy Denean Sharpley-Whiting, and Manthia Diawara. This project also undoubtedly benefited from the attention my editor Eric Zinner at NYU Press who pushed me to develop the central themes of the book.

There are three individuals without whom this book would have been nearly impossible: Thomas Breeze, who engaged me in hours of conversation about hip hop as it is, was, and should be; Talib Shabazz, whose insight is reflected in my writing on the "Old Schools" of the music and whose friendship I've valued since the days of fat laces and pinstripe Lees; and Kamasi Hill, who lent his perspective (as well as his books and music) and listened to endless stream-of-consciousness riffs as ideas came to me on the subject. I hope this book is reflective of the quality of their thinking.

In the South, people have a way of saying "I appreciate you" as a more meaningful replacement for "thank you." In that regard, I *appreciate* my own clan, Mary Cobb, Valerie Foster, Nandi Ayeesha Wright, Tymel Bester, Billy, Terrence and Natasha Foster, Naomi Parker, Ann Adams, Joanne Townsend Gaines, Wellington Hansberry, Rev. Frank Cobb, Charles and Carla Worthy, Chante Roger, Anthony Pratt, Kim Johnson, James (Spike) Johnson, Michael McButts, and Vanessa and James Holmes.

Kristy R. Holley encouraged this project literally five minutes after its conception—at a point when a simple "that's a good idea, you should do it" carries manifold significance. Rhea Combs gave me invaluable support and insisted that I work on this project rather than the dozen others that competed for my attention. Thanks go to Carley Lester for being Carley Lester.

Zenzi Whitsett had the generosity of time and spirit to read this entire manuscript and shared her insights on its improvement with me. I think it's better for her attentions and I am better for knowing her. And while I'm on that subject, I need to acknowledge my peoples Simba, Yao, and Sunny at Karibu Books (www.Karibubooks.com). My regards go to my brothers-in-ink, Kenny Carroll, Joel Dias-Porter, Ta-Nehisi Coates, and Brian Gilmore. The late Ralph Wiley was a cut man and trainer during my early rounds as writer and his presence in my corner will be missed for a long, long while.

Thanks also go to my agent Charlotte Sheedy, as well as Emily Park and Debbie Gershenowitz at NYU Press, Andrew Ryan and the *Journal of Hip Hop*; and my fellow Africana.com columnists, Mark Anthony Neal, Lester Kenyatta Spence, Bethany Allen, and Amy Alexander. I also appreciate Terence Nicholson (Sub-Z), who explained to me the finer points of MCing during our interview on that subject. I've also been informed and inspired by Toni Blackman's work to consistently expand the parameters of hip hop culture.

I have benefited from the insights and friendship of Shani Jamila O'Neal Mali Fleming, D. Natasha Brewley, Khalil Muhammad, Stephanie Lawson-Muhammad, Natasha Tarpley, Charles and Stephanie Wright, and Tiffany Gill. Both my professional and personal admiration go to Arthur Flowers, Robin D. G. Kelley, Byron Hurt, Robyn Spencer, Daryl Scott, Michael Eric Dyson, and David Levering Lewis. Rafi Aliya Crockett contributed to this effort in his own individual way, as did Kila and Jazz at Earwax Records in Atlanta, T. Tara Turk, Cynthia Young, Akanke Washington, Valerie Boyd, Alejandro Bodipo-Memba, and Jodi Merriday. Sherman Brown, Dennis Dobbins, and Mark Mason have been my boys since the tenth grade and I'm glad to still know those brothers. On the subject of allies dating back to the old school—literally—I'd be remiss to not mention Marilyn Johnson, Fred Hanna, and Mike Gumby. Add to that roster of indispensables Lori Robinson, Natalie Bullock-Brown, Damita Coats, Marcia Davis, Fanon Che Wilkins, Shonda Hornbeck, Mia Mitchell, Tomika DePriest, Juliana Montgomery, and my research assistant, Erica Sowell.

I also appreciate the support of my colleagues, Anne Bailey, Dalila DeSousa-Shepard, Margery Ganz, James Gillam, Kathleen Philips-Lewis, Aaron Frith—to whom I'm indebted for use of his collection of Robert Johnson recordings—Sheila Walker and Sharon Washington, who provided invaluable support for my work. I've also benefited from the insights of Dr. Beverly Daniel Tatum and the students in my Topics in Hip Hop Culture class—Alexandria Lee, Nekima Hill, Rebecca Chattman, Amanda Newsome, Mikael Moore, Hafeeza Rashed, Tina Moore, Dana Gabriel, Kelly Mitchell, Nandi Troutman, Keonna Yates, Alisha Gordon, Tomiko Ballantyne-Nisbett, Cristen Mills, Dawn Hazleton, Stacy Carraway, Kia Smith, Shaba Lightfoot, Ashanti Hollingsworth, Jennifer Moore, and Monet Musler—had a hand in the evolution of this project as well, and I eagerly anticipate seeing the brilliance of their own future projects.

In that same vein, big respect goes to the incisive minds at Playahata.com (I swear I'll get to that book review!), as well as those on Sistrumatic and Afrofuturism listservs, especially Chris Cobb, Alondra Nelson, Cinque Hicks, Lynne D. Johnson, Carol Cooper, Harry Allen, Xavier Moon, Chris Hayden, DJ Thorrin, and Khem, whose collective wisdom on this subject—and a whole lot of other subjects—informed my own thinking about hip hop. And special thanks to Shaheen Ariefdien, who shared his bibliography of hip hop with me during a crucial juncture of my work.

I owe a debt of gratitude to the writers—many of whom I know solely as a reader of their words—but whose work has elevated the discussion of hip hop as an art form: Jeff Chang, James Bernard, Joan Morgan, Elizabeth Mendez Berry, Michael Gonzales, Dave Tomkins, Touré, Kelefa Sanneh, Davey D, and Nelson George. A whole lot of these words were written in the Javaology Café on Edgewood and Boulevard in Atlanta (www.javaologyatl.com), where conversations got sparked by overheard statements like "picking cotton was not that big a deal." So I'd be dead-wrong not to shout out the crew there: Morgan, Jennifer, Willis, Sonya, Cameron, Precious, Devin, LeJuano, and Henry. That same note of appreciation goes to Eddie Lovick and the staff of E2 Café in East Atlanta.

And then there are the friends who may not have contributed directly to the book itself, but whose friendship has been a priceless addition to my life nonetheless: Dineo Brinson, Asha Bandele, Derrick Selby, Kenton Clayton, Brentin Mock, Kupenda Auset, Camille Acey, April Silver, Georgene Bess Montgomery, Tonya Bolden, Vanessa Boyd, Jodine Dorce, Damaris Hardiman, Clarence Lusane, Sharon Sanders, Renee Holtz, Elizabeth Clark-Lewis, Marcia Davis, Eric Easter, Indra Tobias, Tiffany Friesen, Travis Ray, Edda Fields-Black, Rich Byers, Regina Rice, Sharan Strange, Thomas Sayers Ellis, Kim Pearson, Stephen Newsome, Gloria Dickinson, Lawrence Jackson, Matthew Williams, Minkah Makalani, Romas Mills, Murithi Alafia, Rob Vincent, and Armand Jones. A note of appreciation goes to Terrence Hayes and Yona Harvey, who, in addition to being skilled wordsmiths in their own right, gave this author a ride to the Pittsburgh airport one bitterly cold night in 2005. A special thanks goes to Ethelbert Miller, who told me "I think you got some books in you, brother" way back in 1993 and inspired me to prove him right. Thanks go to my editors at Africana.com, Kate Tuttle—who initiated my "Past Imperfect" column—Zakia Carter, Tanu Henry, and Gary Dauphin, as well as Victoria Valentine at *Crisis* magazine, Jabari Asim at the *Washington Post*, Diane Weathers and Rosemarie Robotham at *Essence*, Kay Shaw, Ted Shaw, Herschel Johnson, Melissa Woods, Debo Adegbile, Alaina Beverly, and Janai Nelson at the NAACP-LDF, Leah Latimer at Voicesofcivilrights.org, and Leonard Roberge at the *Washington City Paper*.

Finally, I have a tremendous debt of gratitude to Nakia Bazemore, who I had good fortune to work with for four years at Spelman College. She helped this project and its author in innumerable ways. I lament that she did not live to see it in its final form, but her grace, warmth, humor, and intelligence have an enduring space in the hearts of all of us who were blessed to know her.

Notes

vii   *In spite of and because of marginal status* . . . John Edgar Wideman, "Introduction," *Breaking Ice: An Anthology of Contemporary African American Fiction*, New York: Penguin, 1990.

vii   *You criticize our methods/Of how we make records* . . . Stetsasonic, *In Full Gear*, Tommy Boy Records, 2001.

4   *Before we arrive at the mandatory* . . . Franz Fanon, *Wretched of the Earth*, New York: Grove Press, 1965.

4   *Each generation is imbued* . . . See also Brian Cross, *It's Not About a Salary: Rap, Race and Resistance in Los Angeles*, New York: Verso, 1993.

6   *But at the same time, hip hop is not fundamentally* . . . Langston Hughes, "The Negro Artist and the Racial Mountain," in David Levering Lewis (ed), *Harlem Renaissance Reader*, New York: Henry Holt, 1993.

7   *But this new multiculturalism is global and international* . . . W. E. B. Du Bois "Criteria of Negro Art," in David Levering Lewis (ed), *Harlem Renaissance Reader*, New York: Henry Holt, 1993.

8   *The genealogy of the MC* . . . Jim Fricke, *Yes, Yes, Y'all: The Oral History of Hip Hop's First Decade*, Cambridge, MA: Da Capo Press, 2002.

10   *So this book aims for a different* . . . Though most of the literature on hip hop has concentrated on its social politics, the aesthetic principles over the music have been ably discussed in Tricia Rose's *Black Noise: Rap Music and Black Culture in Contemporary America*, Middletown, CT: Wesleyan University Press, 1994; Imani Perry's *Prophets of the Hood: Politics and Poetics in Hip Hop*, Durham: Duke University Press, 2004; and scholarly articles—particularly Geneva Smitherman's "The Chain Remain the Same" (*Journal of Black Studies*,

September 1997) and Mtume ya Salaam's "The Aesthetics of Rap" (*African American Review*, Summer 1995).

15   *Our preachers are talented men* . . . Carla Kaplan, *Zora Neale Hurston: A Life in Letters*, New York: Anchor Books, 2003.

15   *The Black preacher, since the church* . . . James Baldwin, *Evidence of Things Not Seen*, New York: Owl Books, 1995.

16   *Listen for a minute and it becomes clear* . . . Michael Eric Dyson, *Between God and Gangsta Rap: Bearing Witness to Black Culture*, New York: Oxford University Press, 1997. Also, Anthony Pinn, *Noise and Spirit: The Religious and Spiritual Sensibilities of Rap Music*, New York: NYU Press, 2003. The significance of hooping to black rhetorical style was emphasized to me in discussion on the subject with Kamasi Hill and Christina Dickerson.

17   *Of those multiple millions of Africans* . . . Regarding the relationship between dancehall and hip hop, see Jeff Chang, *Can't Stop Won't Stop: A History of the Hip Hop Generation*, New York: St. Martin's Press, 2005. Joseph Holloway, *Africanisms in American Culture*, Bloomington: Indiana University Press, 1991. Regarding the percentages of enslaved Africans brought to North America, see Philip Curtin's *TransAtlantic Slave Trade: A Census*, Madison: University of Wisconsin Press, 1997. See also David Eltis, *Routes to Slavery; Direction, Ethnicity and Mortality in the Transatlantic Slave Trade*, London: Frank Cass, 1997.

19   *To the enslaved, though, to the African* . . . On this subject, see LeRoi Jones, *Blues People: Negro Music in White America*, New York: Harper Perennial, 1999.

19   *Forbidden to seek communion and connection* . . . For discussion of the subject of slave conversion to Christianity, see Albert Raboteau, *Slave Religion: The Invisible Institution in the Antebellum South*, New York: Oxford University Press, 2004. See also LeRoi Jones's *Blues People*.

20   *The blank-faced, cinema verité* . . . Jon Michael Spencer, *Blues and Evil*, Knoxville: University of Tennessee Press, 1993.

20   *Literary bluesman and musician* . . . Ralph Ellison, *Shadow and Act*, New York: Vintage, 1995, 78.

21   *The trickster's ironic sensibility* . . . Robert D. Pelton, *The Trickster in West Africa: A Study of Mythic Irony and Sacred Delight*, Berkeley: University of California Press, 1980.

22   *The Dogon imagination* . . . Pelton, 219.

23   *Westerners have conflated Elegba the trickster* . . . On this subject see Robert Farris Thompson, *Flash of the Spirit: African and Afro-American Art and Philosophy*, New York: Vintage, 1984; Spencer, *Blues and Evil*; and Julio Finn, *The Bluesman: The Musical Heritage of Black Men and Women in the Americas*, London: Quartet Press, 1987.

25   *Fruit may not fall far from the tree* . . . Regarding the number of blues songs discussing travel, see Michael Taft, *Blues Lyric Poetry: A Concordance*, New York: Garland Publishing, 1984. Regarding space and locality in hip hop, see also Imani Perry, *Prophets of the Hood*, Durham: Duke University Press, 2004; and Murray Forman, *The Hood Comes First: Race, Space and Place in Rap and Hip Hop*, Middletown, CT: Wesleyan University Press, 2002.

28   *I was like totally wack on the mic* . . . Fricke, *Yes, Yes, Y'all*.

28   *The most apparent survivals* . . . Jones, *Blues People*, 25.

32   *Georgia, 1899* . . . Philip Dray, *At the Hands of Persons Unknown: The Lynching of Black America*, New York: Random House, 2002, 18.

33   *Jack Trice fought fifteen white men* . . . Herbert Aptheker, *Documentary History of the Negro People in the United States*, Volume II, New York: Citadel, 1973, 795.

34   *The two most identifiable American folk heroes* . . . A fuller discussion of this theme is found in Robert Warshow's noted essays "The Gangster as Tragic Hero" and "The Westerner" in *The Immediate Experience: Movies, Comics, Theatre and Other Aspects of Popular Culture*, Cambridge, MA: Harvard University Press, 2002.

35   *I pointed out earlier that the Baaad Nigger* . . . Regarding blues significance to black women, see Angela Davis, *Blues Legacies and Black Feminism*, New York: Pantheon, 1998. See also Farah Griffin, *If You Can't Be Free, Be a Mystery: In Search of Billie Holiday*, New York: One World, 2002. See Darlene Clark Hine regarding the Great Migration and Black Women, "Black Migration to the Urban Midwest: The Gender Dimension," in Joe William Trotter (ed), *The Great Migration in Historical Perspective*, Bloomington: University of Indiana Press, 1991.

36   *One of the most prevalent images of black women* . . . The "Jezebel" figure is the focus of an entire chapter of Deborah White's *Ar'n't I A Woman: Female Slaves in the Plantation South*, New York: Norton, 1999.

41   *As an MC You will Study* . . . KRS-ONE, "The MC" *I Got Next*, Jive Records, 1997.

42   *In those earliest days* . . . For more on the relationship of hip hop to the Black Arts Movement, see Marvin Gladney, "The Black Arts Movement and Hip Hop," in *African American Review* (Summer 1995).

43   *There was nothing in rap like that except the Last Poets* . . . *The Sugar Hill Story*, Sugar Hill Records, 1991, liner notes, 32.

46   *Hip Hop was that joy* . . . For further discussion of the importance of this early politicization of the music, see Yvonne Bynoe, *Stand and Deliver: Political Activism, Leadership and Hip Hop*, Brooklyn: Soft Skull Press, 2003; and Bakari Kitwana, *The Hip Hop Generation*, New York: Basic Books, 2002. For a discussion of Melle Mel's artistic importance, check Kool Moe Dee's *There's a God on the Mic: The True 50 Greatest MCs*, New York: Thunder's Mouth, 2003.

48   *The thematic boundaries of what constituted* . . . The gender politics of hip hop have been analyzed thoroughly—particularly in Joan Morgan's groundbreaking *When Chickenheads Come Home to Roost*, New York: Simon & Schuster, 2000; as well as later works, including Gwendolyn Pough's *Check It While I Wreck It: Black Womanhood, Hip Hop Culture and the Public Sphere*, Boston: Northeastern University Press, 2004; and Charise Cheney, *Brothers Gonna Work It Out: Sexual Politics in the Golden Age of Rap Nationalism*, New York: NYU Press, 2005.

49   *From the gate there had been females present within the cipher* . . . In more recent years, this point was rearticulated not only by hip hop scholars, but also by performance artists/MCs like Toni Blackman and Kim Ellis (Dr. Goddess).

49   *As early as 1980, the Sequence* . . . For an additional discussion on the early presence of female MCs, see Fricke, *Yes, Yes, Y'all*.

51   *At the same time, the outlets responsible* . . . An excellent discussion of the role of indie labels in the birth and early development of recorded hip hop is seen in Salaam, "The Aesthetics of Rap."

52   *It was during this point that hip hop also came to sound different* . . . More on this in Rose's *Black Noise* and Bill Brewster and Frank Broughton's *Last Night a DJ Saved My Life: A History of the Disc Jockey*, New York: Grove Press, 2000.

53 . . . *was still current enough to prompt Talib Kweli to point out* . . . Author's
interview with Talib Kweli, April 2004.

54 *The Ultra Magnetics debut release* . . . In what is easily one of the best pieces
of hip hop journalism yet produced, Dave Tomkins's "Traveling At The Speed
of Thought" charts the life, work, and musical significance of Paul C.—a producer whose artistic brilliance has been overshadowed by his premature and
mysterious death. See
http://crunkster.abstractdynamics.org/archives/003807.html.

55 *To be accurate, though, by the 1980s R&B was a wasteland* . . . See Nelson
George, *Death of Rhythm and Blues*, New York: Pantheon Books, 1988.

57 *In Cali context*, Dr. Dre's 1992 solo debut. . . see William Shaw, *Westside:
Young Men and Hip Hop in L.A.*, New York: Simon & Schuster, 2000.

58 *But this self-titled debut* . . . See Oliver Wang (ed), *Classic Material: The Hip-
Hop Album Guide*, Toronto: ECW Press, 2003, 52.

58 *The unstated element* . . . *was their background as Latino artists* . . . Regarding
Latino influence in hip hop, see "It's a Street Thing: Charlie Chase Interview,"
Callaloo, Vol. 15, No. 4 (Autumn, 1992); Raquel Rivera, *New York Ricans From
the Hip Hop Zone*, New York: Palgrave, 2003, Juan Flores, *From Bomba to Hip
Hop: Puerto Rican Culture and Latino Identity*, New York: Columbia University
Press, 2000.

61 *The dominant element of that era* . . . see Chuck D., *Fight the Power: Rap, Race,
and Reality*, New York: Delacorte, 1997.

63 *The Chronic marked the ascent* . . . For a detailed examination of the rise of
West Coast hip hop, particularly Death Row Records, see Ronin Ro's excellent
Have Gun Will Travel, Pella, IA: Main Street Books, 1999.

64 *Similarly, Too Short* . . . See Vladimir Bogdanov (ed), *All Music Guide to
Hip-Hop: The Definite Guide to Rap and Hip-Hop*, San Francisco: Backbeat Books,
2003.

65 *Gangsta—as the media termed the dawning movement* . . . The significance of
this, particularly its socio-historical context, is seen in Robin D. G. Kelley's
"Kickin Reality, Kickin Ballistics," in his collection *Race Rebels*, New York: Free
Press, 1996.

180 NOTES

67   *Deciphering Wu-Tang was as simple as reading Braille hieroglyphics* . . . The Wu-Tang cosmology is broken down by RZA himself in *The Wu-Tang Manual,* New York: Riverhead Trade, 2004.

71   *Whatever the case was to become, the Nas of Illmatic* . . . Wang, *Classic Material.*

71   *Clitoral shtick became central to the female artists.* . . For more, check Cheney, *Brothers Gonna Work It Out.*

73   *That Tupac had elusively managed to become the most revered* . . . See Michael Eric Dyson, *Holler If You Hear Me: Searching for Tupac Shakur,* New York: Basic Books, 2001.

77   *Rapper grips mic tight* . . . Joel Dias-Porter, untitled poem, unpublished, 1995.

77   *The practice of mother-rhyming has been observed in various Afro-American communities* . . . Abrahams, *African American Folktales: Stories from Black Traditions in the New World,* New York: Pantheon, 1999, 64.

78   *When confined to friends and familiar circumstances* . . . Mel Watkins, *On the Real Side: A History of African American Comedy,* New York: Simon & Schuster, 1994, 455.

79   *Once I saw a prizefighter boxing a yokel* . . . Ralph Ellison, *Invisible Man,* New York: Vintage, 1972, 8.

79   *People compare rap to other genres of music* . . . Jay-Z interview, *Vibe Magazine,* January 2004.

79   *If Liston had not been born* . . . Check Nick Tosches, *The Devil and Sonny Liston,* New York: Back Bay Books: 2001.

86   *The Kool Herc style at the time* . . . Fricke, *Yes, Yes, Y'all,* 71.

86   *R&B is black music*...Big Daddy Kane, www.halftimeonline.com/kane.html.

89   *In this case, the punchline is technically the third* . . . Regarding the blues poetic structure, see Taft, *Blues Lyric Poetry: An Anthology.*

107   *Those of us who have learned to write from the blues* . . : Murray Kempton, "Bessie Smith: Poet," in *Rebellions, Perversities and Main Events,* New York: Three Rivers Press, 1995.

109 *A person inherits compulsive instincts* . . . M. H. Abrams, *Glossary of Literary Terms*, Boston: Heinle Press, 1998; see also Kelley, "Kickin Reality, Kickin Ballistics."

110 *A master performance artist* . . . Quote from Touré, "Tupac Shakur Gives the Performance of His Life," *Village Voice*, December 13, 1994.

110 *The world now consumes films, novels, theater* . . . Robert Mckee, *Story*, New York: Regan Books, 1997.

111 *The changes that freedom wrought* . . . Lawrence Levine, *Black Culture, Black Consciousness*, New York: Oxford University Press, 1978, 369–70.

111 *Heroism, which is, among other things, another word for self-reliance* . . . Albert Murray, *Hero and the Blues*, New York: Vintage, 1996, 44.

112 *This is a culture that, on the level of its stylistic temperature* . . . Kelley, "Kickin Reality, Kickin Ballistics"; Wesley Brown, *Stagolee Shot Billy*, Cambridge, MA: Harvard University Press, 2003, 220.

115 *As an oral performance, Stagolee has influenced a new art form* . . . Brown, *Stagolee Shot Billy*, 225.

117 *The "cult of the gunfighter" is constituted* . . . Richard Slotkin, *Gunfighter Nation: The Myth of the Frontier in 20th Century America*, Norman: University of Oklahoma Press, 402.

119 *It was Saturday night and the jungle was bright* . . . Wepman, Newman & Binderman (eds) *The Life: The Lore and Folk Poetry of the Black Hustler*, Los Angeles: Holloway House Publishing, 1976. 89–100.

120 *I gave her a way-out funeral and didn't spare no cash* . . . Wepman, et al., *The Life*, 48.

121 *And while Miles confessed to pimping during his heroin daze* . . . Robin D. G. Kelley, "Miles Davis: The Chameleon of Cool; A Jazz Genius in the Guise of a Hustler," *New York Times*, May 13, 2001.

122 *We Real Cool* . . . Gwendolyn Brooks, in Henry Louis Gates Jr. and Nellie Y. Mckay (eds), *The Norton Anthology of African American Literature*, New York: Norton, 1997, 1591.

131 *In late 1934, I would guess, something began to happen* . . . Malcolm X and Alex Haley, *The Autobiography of Malcolm X*, New York: Ballantine Books, 1987, 18.

133 *The pimps would sidle up close* . . . Malcolm X, *Autobiography*, 87.

134 *I preferred the solitary that this behavior brought me* . . . Malcolm X, *Autobiography*, 177.

136 *I have rarely talked to anyone about my mother* . . . Malcolm X, *Autobiography*, 27.

139 *I take seven MCs, put 'em in a line* . . . Like Muhammad Ali, Rakim has consistently brought out the best in the scribes that have taken him up as a subject. He is the subject of an excellent analysis by Mark Anthony Neal, " . . . And Bless the Mic for the Gods: Rakim Allah," *Pop Matters*, November 19, 2003, http://www.popmatters.com/music/features/031119-rakim.shtml; see also Bogdanov (ed), *All Music Guide*; as well as Rob Marriott's brilliant "Allah's on Me," in Raquel Cepeda's *And It Don't Stop: The Best American Hip Hop Journalism of the Last 25 Years*, New York: Faber & Faber, 2004.

147 *For black men, beseeching America to recognize* . . . On the subject of the meaning and implications of Jay-Z's music and career, see Elizabeth Mendez Berry, "Hard Knock Life, Vol. 1" in Wang, *Classic Material*, 93–96.

157 *In the pantheon of disposable American heroes* . . . See Hilton Als and Daryl Turner (eds), *White Nose: The Eminem Collection*, New York: Thunder's Mouth, 2003.

163 *Brooklyn death-angels came draped* . . . For more, see Cheo Hodari Coker's *Unbelievable: The Life, Death and Afterlife of Notorious B.I.G.*, New York: Plexus, 2004.

168 *It is at these times* . . . Eileen Southern, *The Music of Black Americans: A History*, New York: Norton, 1997, 609.

Index

About the Author

William Jelani Cobb is Assistant Professor of History at Spelman College and the editor of *The Essential Harold Cruse: A Reader.* He resides in Atlanta, Georgia. His Web site can be found at www.jelanicobb.com.